STEAMING BASICS

MY COOKING CLASS

STEAMING BASICS
97 RECIPES ILLUSTRATED
STEP BY STEP

ORATHAY GUILLAUMONT

PHOTOGRAPHS BY PIERRE JAVELLE

❋ ❋ ❋

FIREFLY BOOKS

A FIREFLY BOOK

Published by Firefly Books Ltd. 2010

First printing

Publisher Cataloging-in-Publication Data (U.S.)
Guillaumont, Orathay.
    Steaming basics : 97 recipes illustrated step by step / Orathay Guillaumont ;
photographs by Pierre Javelle.
[256] p. : col. photos. ;   cm.
Includes index.
ISBN-13: 978-1-55407-757-1 (pbk.)
ISBN-10: 1-55407-757-5 (pbk.)
1. Steaming (Cookery). I. Javelle, Pierre. II. Title.
641.73 dc22   TX691.G855 2010

Library and Archives Canada Cataloguing in Publication
Guillaumont, Orathay
    Steaming basics : 97 recipes illustrated step by step / Orathay Guillaumont.
Includes index.
ISBN-13: 978-1-55407-757-1 (pbk.)
ISBN-10: 1-55407-757-5 (pbk.)
    1. Steaming (Cookery). I. Title.
TX691.G85 2010   641.5'87   C2010-901566-5

Published in the United States by
Firefly Books (U.S.) Inc.
P.O. Box 1338, Ellicott Station
Buffalo, New York 14205

Published in Canada by
Firefly Books Ltd.
66 Leek Crescent
Richmond Hill, Ontario L4B 1H1

Printed in China

PREFACE

~~~~~~

In your hands you are holding 97 no-fail steaming recipes, from exotic Asian creations to reinvented classics. Whether you are a beginner or an experienced home cook, you will definitely find a recipe that works for you.

Illustrations guide you through each important step, so you'll be able to successfully prepare every recipe. Dim sums, the classics of Chinese cooking, are revealed step by step: learn how shrimp dumplings, pork bites and Chinese buns are actually prepared.

Rediscover steamed potatoes, accompanied by whipped cream or flavored butters. Prepare a guinea-fowl ballotine for a special meal or invite your friends to gather around party dips, Thai sauce, garlic sauce and tapenade. You'll quickly notice that steaming can be just as gourmet as it is accessible.

✳ ✳ ✳

CONTENTS

CONDIMENTS

SEASONINGS

FLAVORED BUTTERS

SAUCES

THAI SAUCE

➤ YIELD: ABOUT 1/3 CUP (75 ML) • PREPARATION: 10 MINUTES ➤

2 tablespoons (30 ml) confectioners' sugar
2 limes, juiced
2 tablespoons (30 ml) fish sauce

3 garlic cloves
Red chili pepper, to taste
Salt, to taste

1 tablespoon (15 ml) chopped cilantro,
optional

1 2
3 4

1	Dilute the sugar with the lime juice and fish sauce.	2	Chop the garlic and chili pepper. Remove the seeds from the chili if you prefer a milder sauce.
3	Add the garlic and the pepper to the lime juice mixture. Taste then adjust the seasoning: the sauce must be acidic, sweet and salty at the same time.	4	Do not add the cilantro until ready to serve. The sauce can be stored for several weeks in a sealed container in the refrigerator. It goes well with fish and seafood.

GARLIC OIL

➤ YIELD: 1 CUP (250 ML) • PREPARATION: 20 MINUTES • COOKING: 10 MINUTES ➤

1 garlic head
1 cup (250 ml) vegetable oil (canola or
sunflower)

TIP:
Garlic oil is an indispensable condiment in
Asian cooking. It's used to flavor vegetables,

fish, meat and noodles. One or two
tablespoons are enough to season a dish.

1	Peel the garlic cloves and chop with a Chinese cleaver or chef's knife.	2	Heat the oil over medium heat. Once it is hot, add the garlic and lower the heat to minimum.
3	Once the garlic starts to brown, remove the pan from the heat. The oil is still hot and will continue to cook the garlic.	4	Once the garlic oil has cooled, transfer it to a jar. This oil will keep for several weeks at room temperature and almost indefinitely in the refrigerator.

FRENCH WEST INDIAN "SAUCE CHIEN"

➤ YIELD: ABOUT 1 CUP (250 ML) • PREPARATION: 10 MINUTES ➤

1 tomato
2 green onions, preferably large and mature
½ bunch flat-leaf parsley

1 garlic clove
½ ounce (10 g) fresh ginger
2 red chili peppers or ½ habanero chili

2 limes, juiced
Salt & pepper, to taste
⅔ cup (150 ml) boiling water

1 2
3 4

1	Seed and finely dice the tomato. Mince the green onions.	2	Finely slice the parsley and finely chop the garlic, ginger and peppers.
3	Mix all of the ingredients from steps 1 and 2 in a bowl and add the lime juice. Season with salt and pepper.	4	Pour the boiling water over the ingredients in the bowl. Cover immediately with plastic wrap and set aside at room temperature. Taste and adjust the seasoning as needed when ready to serve.

HERB BUTTER

⇢ **YIELD: ABOUT 1 CUP (250 ML) • PREPARATION: 10 MINUTES** ⇠

1 shallot
2 garlic cloves
½ bunch flat-leaf parsley
½ bunch chives
1 cup (250 ml) butter, softened
Salt & pepper, to taste

Mince the shallot, garlic and the herbs. Mix all of the ingredients and season with salt and pepper. Roll up the herb butter in plastic wrap and refrigerate.

TIP:

Once the herb butter has hardened, cut into sections, wrap in plastic wrap and freeze in individual servings.

CITRUS BUTTER

❧ **YIELD: 1 CUP (250 ML)** • **PREPARATION: 30 MINUTES** ❧

Zest (blanched and chopped) and juice from
2 oranges, 1 small grapefruit & 1 lemon
1 tablespoon (15 ml) sugar
1 tablespoon (15 ml) whole-grain mustard
1 cup (250 ml) butter, softened
Salt & pepper, to taste

Over medium heat, reduce the citrus juice by half, along with the sugar. Mix the reduced juice and the zest with the mustard and butter.

Season with salt and pepper. Roll up the citrus butter in plastic wrap and store in the refrigerator.

ALMOND-LEMON BUTTER

➤ **YIELD: ABOUT 1 CUP (250 ML)** • **PREPARATION: 5 MINUTES** ➤

1½ ounces (40 g) roasted unsalted almonds,
  finely chopped
2 lemons, zested and 1 juiced
1 cup (250 ml) butter, softened
Salt & pepper, to taste

Mix the ingredients and season
with salt and pepper. Roll up
in plastic wrap and store in the
refrigerator.

TOMATO-BASIL BUTTER

❧ YIELD: 1 CUP (250 ML) • PREPARATION: 10 MINUTES ❧

1¾ ounces (50 g) grated Parmesan (about ⅓ cup/75 ml)
2 ounces (60 g) roasted tomatoes, chopped
1 bunch basil, chopped
1 cup (250 ml) butter, softened

1 tablespoon (15 ml) whole-grain mustard
1 teaspoon (5 ml) hot paprika
Salt, to taste

Mix the Parmesan, tomatoes and basil into the butter. Add the mustard, season with salt and paprika and mix. Roll up in plastic wrap and refrigerate.

HOLLANDAISE SAUCE

❧ **YIELD: ABOUT ¾ CUP (175 ML)** • PREPARATION: 15 MINUTES • COOKING: 5 MINUTES ❧

1 cup (250 ml) butter
3 egg yolks
2 tablespoons (30 ml) water

½ lemon
Salt, to taste

TIPS: This sauce complements white or green asparagus perfectly, and it is delicious with fish and white meats.

1 2
3 4

1	Melt the butter. Clarify by removing the foam that forms on the surface and gently pouring the melted butter into a bowl, taking care not to pour in the whey (the cloudy deposit at the bottom).	2	In a saucepan, whisk the yolks with the water over very low heat until the temperature reaches 120 to 130°F (50 to 55°C). The yolks must have a foamy consistency.
3	Remove from the heat and gradually add the clarified butter.	4	Add the lemon juice and season with salt. Use immediately or place plastic wrap directly on top of the sauce, store in the refrigerator and reheat in a double boiler.

MOUSSELINE SAUCE

VARIATION OF HOLLANDAISE SAUCE
❋

To make a lighter, airier sauce, add whipped cream to hollandaise sauce. Measure about ½ the volume of the sauce, or ½ cup (125 ml) of heavy (whipping) cream for 1 cup (250 ml) of sauce.

TIPS: This sauce complements white or green asparagus perfectly, and it is delicious with fish and white meats.

MALTAISE SAUCE

VARIATION OF HOLLANDAISE SAUCE

❊

To prepare a maltaise sauce, reduce the juice of 2 oranges by half and mix into a hollandaise sauce, at the same time as the lemon juice. You can also zest the oranges, blanche the zest and add it to the sauce.

TIPS: Maltaise sauce can accompany hot appetizers or side dishes (such as asparagus), fish and white meats.

MAYONNAISE

✤ YIELD: ABOUT 1¼ CUPS (310 ML) • PREPARATION: 10 MINUTES ✤

2 egg yolks
1 teaspoon (5 ml) mustard, optional
Salt & pepper, to taste

1 cup (250 ml) vegetable oil (canola,
   sunflower or grapeseed)
1 dash lemon juice or vinegar

LIGHT MAYONNAISE:
Substitute 3½ ounces (100 g) whipped
fromage blanc (or Greek-style yogurt or
cream cheese) for the oil.

1 2
3 4

1	Put the egg yolks, mustard, salt and pepper in a bowl.	2	Begin whisking then gradually drizzle the oil into the mixture, whisking to incorporate it. The mixture will thicken.
3	Gradually drizzle in the rest of the oil, whisking continuously. Add the lemon juice and adjust the seasoning.	4	Place plastic wrap directly on top of the mayonnaise (so it doesn't form a skin), and store in the refrigerator for up to 1 day.

CILANTRO–CHILI PEPPER MAYONNAISE

VARIATION OF MAYONNAISE
❋

Prepare a batch of mayonnaise (see recipe 11). Mince the leaves from ½ bunch cilantro, zest 1 lime and mix both into the mayonnaise.

Season with the juice of half a lemon and some hot pepper flakes. Taste and adjust the seasoning as needed.

COCKTAIL SAUCE

VARIATION OF MAYONNAISE

To prepare a cocktail sauce, add 3 tablespoons (45 ml) ketchup, 2 tablespoons (30 ml) whiskey and a dash of Tabasco sauce to a batch of mayonnaise (see recipe 11).

For a lighter version, substitute 3½ ounces (100 g) whipped fromage blanc, Greek-style yogurt or light cream cheese for the mayonnaise and add 1 teaspoon (5 ml) hot mustard.

AIOLI

❖ YIELD: ABOUT 1 CUP (250 ML) • PREPARATION: 15 MINUTES ❖

1 potato (about 3 ounces/80 g)
2 to 4 garlic cloves, to taste
Coarse salt, to taste
2 egg yolks
½ lemon, juiced
⅔ cup (150 ml) olive oil

PRELIMINARY:
Steam or boil the potato with the skin on.
Peel it and allow it to cool.

TIP:
Blanch the garlic cloves for a milder aioli.

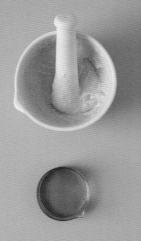

1	Peel the garlic cloves, place in a mortar with a pinch of coarse salt and the cooked potato. Mash with a pestle.	2	Add the egg yolks and mix with the pestle. Add the lemon juice and mix again.
3	Gradually drizzle in the olive oil, continuously stirring with the pestle.	4	Stir continuously until the aioli is firm. Taste and adjust the seasoning if necessary. Cover with plastic wrap and set aside at room temperature.

ANCHOVY PASTE

❧ YIELD: ABOUT 1 CUP (250 ML) • PREPARATION: 10 MINUTES ❧

7 ounces (200 g) anchovies in oil
1 ounce (30 g) black olives, pitted
1 small bunch basil, washed and stems
   removed
1 cup (250 ml) olive oil
½ lemon, juiced

2 garlic cloves, peeled, halved and germs
   removed
Pepper, to taste

In a blender or food processor, blend
everything except the pepper until you
obtain a uniform and smooth sauce.
Season with pepper. Serve immediately or
cover with plastic wrap and refrigerate.

TAPENADE

❧ **YIELD: ABOUT 1½ CUPS (375 ML) • PREPARATION: 5 MINUTES** ❧

14 ounces (400 g) black olives, pitted
10 anchovies in oil
1 tablespoon (15 ml) capers
1 garlic clove, peeled, halved and germ removed
2 tablespoons (30 ml) sherry vinegar

In a blender or food processor, blend until you obtain a uniform sauce. Serve immediately or cover with plastic wrap and refrigerate.

If the tapenade is too thick, thin with a little olive oil.

LIGHT TARTAR SAUCE

➤ YIELD: ABOUT 1 CUP (250 ML) • PREPARATION: 15 MINUTES ➤

1 shallot
Few springs parsley, chives & chervil
2 egg yolks, hard-boiled
5 ounces (150 g) whipped fromage blanc
   (or Greek-style yogurt or cream cheese)

1 teaspoon (5 ml) hot mustard
Salt & pepper, to taste

CLASSIC TARTAR SAUCE:
Replace the fromage blanc with a batch of
mayonnaise (see recipe 11).

1 2
3 4

1	Mince the shallot and the herbs.	2	Mash the egg yolks with a fork.
3	Gradually mix the fromage blanc and mustard into the yolks. Stir until you obtain a uniform sauce.	4	Season with salt and pepper and add the shallot and herbs. You can also add a few chopped pickles and the hard-boiled egg whites. Serve the tartar sauce as a dip for raw vegetables or as a sauce for white meats.

TZATZIKI

❧ **YIELD: ABOUT 1¼ (310 ML) • PREPARATION: 20 MINUTES** ❧

1 cucumber
1 small garlic clove
½ bunch mint

10½ ounces (300 g) Greek yogurt or light
    cream cheese (about 1 cup/250 ml)
1 tablespoon (15 ml) red wine vinegar or
    lemon juice

2 tablespoons (30 ml) olive oil
Salt & pepper, to taste

1 2
3 4

1	Peel, seed and finely slice the cucumber.	2	Allow to drain for 10 minutes in a strainer with a little salt.
3	Finely chop the garlic and mince the mint. Squeeze any excess liquid from the cucumber, and mix it with the garlic, the mint and the rest of the ingredients. Season with salt and pepper.	4	The tzatziki is best served fresh. Serve with vegetables as an appetizer or with fish or meat.

DIM SUM

DUMPLINGS & BITES

SMALL DISHES

SHRIMP FILLING

❖ YIELD: ABOUT 10½ OUNCES (300 G) • PREPARATION: 15 MINUTES ❖

1 ounce (30 g) water chestnuts
1¾ ounces (50 g) bamboo shoots
9 ounces (250 g) shrimp, shelled
1 tablespoon (15 ml) oyster sauce

1 tablespoon (15 ml) soy sauce
1 teaspoon (5 ml) sugar
½ teaspoon (2 ml) salt
Pepper, to taste

1 egg white
2 tablespoons (30 ml) rice wine
1 tablespoon (15 ml) tapioca flour

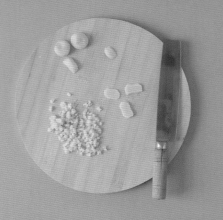

1 2
3 4

1	Finely dice the water chestnuts or chop in a food processor.	2	Coarsely chop the bamboo shoots and half of the shrimp.
3	In a food processor, blend the remaining shrimp with the sauces, sugar, salt, pepper, egg white, rice wine and tapioca flour.	4	Blend until you obtain a uniform filling. Cover with plastic wrap and let rest for 15 minutes before using. The filling can be prepared up to 2 days in advance.

SHRIMP DUMPLINGS

❖ YIELD: 40 DUMPLINGS • PREPARATION: 40 MINUTES • COOKING: 5 MINUTES ❖

FOR THE DOUGH:
1⅓ cup (325 ml) wheat starch (available in Asian supermarkets)
¼ cup (60 ml) tapioca flour

1 pinch salt
⅞ cup (200 ml) boiling water
2 tablespoons (30 ml) canola oil

FILLING:
10½ ounces (300 g) shrimp filling (see recipe 19)

1 2
3 4

1	Mix the wheat starch, tapioca flour and salt. Pour in the boiling water and add the canola oil. Mix using a wooden spatula.	2	Transfer the hot dough to a board and knead for 5 minutes, until the dough is smooth. It should be soft but not sticky.	
3	Roll up sections of dough and slice into ½-inch (1 cm) pieces (about ⅓ ounce/10 g in weight). Keep the dough under plastic wrap to so it doesn't dry out.	4	Roll out the dough between 2 sheets of parchment paper, and cut out circles using a 3-inch (8 cm) diameter cookie cutter.	➢

| 5 | Pleat half the circle of each pastry wrapper to form a pouch, working from the left if you are right-handed and from the right if you are left-handed. Fill each pouch with a teaspoon (5 ml) of filling then pinch together to seal the dumplings. | **OPTION** ❋ You can also fold the pastry circles in half, without making any pleats. This creates croissant-shaped dumplings (see recipe 26). |

6	Steam for 5 minutes in an oiled steamer basket.	**TIP** ❈
		☛ You can also use a packaged mix of flours, ready to use to make Chinese dumplings. Mixes are sold in Asian supermarkets.
	SERVING SUGGESTION ❈	
	The dumplings can be served with a spicy sauce (such as Sriracha sauce) and soy sauce.	

CARROT & SHRIMP BALLS

❧ YIELD: ABOUT 20 TO 25 BALLS • PREPARATION: 30 MINUTES • COOKING: 6 MINUTES ❧

2 carrots
1 small bunch cilantro
7 ounces (200 g) shrimp filling
(see recipe 19)

VARIATION:
You can substitute diced zucchini for the
carrots.

1	Peel and finely dice the carrots. Mince the cilantro.	2	Roll about a teaspoon (5 ml) of shrimp filling into a ball and roll the ball in the diced carrots and the cilantro. Repeat until all the ingredients are used.
3	Place the balls in a steamer basket and steam over high heat for 6 minutes.	4	They're ready! Serve with soy sauce.

SHRIMP WONTON DUMPLINGS

❖ **YIELD: ABOUT 20 DUMPLINGS** • PREPARATION: 30 MINUTES • COOKING: 6 TO 7 MINUTES ❖

10½ ounces (300 g) shrimp filling
  (see recipe 19)
20 wonton skins

TIP:
Shape the wonton dumplings as desired:
join opposite corners to create triangles, or
fold over the edges to form little tarts.

1 2
3 4

1	Working one dumpling at a time, moisten the edges of a wonton skin and place a little filling (about 1 teaspoon/5 ml) in the center. Take care to leave enough space to fold over the edges of the wonton skin.	2	Fold the edges of the wonton skin over the filling. Stick the pastry together by pinching and forming pleats. Follow the same steps for every dumpling.
3	Steam for 6 to 7 minutes over high heat in an oiled steamer basket.	4	They're ready! Serve with spicy Sriracha sauce.

PORK FILLING

❧ YIELD: ABOUT 1 POUND (500 G) • PREPARATION: 15 MINUTES ❧

3½ ounces (100 g) water chestnuts
1 onion
6 green onions
1 ounce (20 g) fresh ginger
1 pound (500 g) ground pork loin

2 tablespoons (30 ml) rice wine
2 tablespoons (30 ml) soy sauce
1 tablespoon (15 ml) sesame oil
½ teaspoon (2 ml) salt

2 tablespoons (30 ml) tapioca flour or
   cornstarch
1 egg white

1 2
3 4

1	Finely dice the water chestnuts or blend in a food processor.	2	Mince the onion, finely slice the green onions and grate the ginger.
3	Mix all of the ingredients in a bowl.	4	Let rest 10 to 15 minutes in the refrigerator before using.

LION'S HEAD MEATBALLS

❖ **YIELD: ABOUT 20 MEATBALLS** • **PREPARATION: 30 MINUTES** • **SOAKING: 2 HOURS** • **COOKING: 8 MINUTES** ❖

½ cup (125 ml) uncooked sticky rice
5 dried shiitake mushrooms
7 ounces (200 g) pork filling (see recipe 23)

PRELIMINARY:
Soak the sticky rice in cold water for at least 2 hours. Rehydrate the shiitake mushrooms by soaking them in cold water for 15 minutes.

1 2
3 4

1	Drain the rice in a strainer and allow to dry for 10 to 15 minutes.	2	Squeeze any excess water from the mushrooms then finely dice them.
3	Mix the diced mushrooms with the pork filling. Shape small balls, and then roll them in the sticky rice.	4	Arrange the meatballs in a steamer basket and steam for 8 minutes over high heat.

XIUMAI PORK BITES

❖ **YIELD: ABOUT 30 BITES** • **PREPARATION: 30 MINUTES** • **COOKING: 7 MINUTES** ❖

1 pound (500 g) ground pork loin
3½ ounces (100 g) water chestnuts
1 onion
6 green onions
1 ounce (20 g) fresh ginger

2 tablespoons (30 ml) rice wine
2 tablespoons (30 ml) soy sauce
1 tablespoon (15 ml) sesame oil
½ teaspoon (2 ml) salt

2 tablespoons (30 ml) tapioca flour or
   cornstarch
1 egg white
1 package wonton skins

1 2
3 4

1	Prepare the meat filling as indicated in recipe 23, beginning with finely chopping all the vegetables.	2	Add the vegetables and the rest of the ingredients to the meat, mix and then set aside.	
3	Separate any wonton skins that are stuck together. Cut circles out of the wonton skins with a 3-inch (8 cm) diameter cookie cutter.	4	Drop about a teaspoon (5 ml) of filling in the middle of each wonton circle.	➤

5	Moisten the edges of the wonton circle with a little water using a pastry brush, fold the wonton around the filling and seal by lightly pressing the edges together.	**SHRIMP VARIATION** ❉ Substitute 8 ounces (250 g) shrimps for 8 ounces (250 g) ground pork and blend in a food processor until you obtain a slightly sticky mixture. Add the rest of the ingredients for the filling and mix by hand.

| 6 | Steam for 5 to 7 minutes in an oiled steamer basket. Serve these bites with soy sauce and Sriracha sauce. | **TIP** ❊

These pork bites freeze well, so don't hesitate to make a double recipe. Cook from frozen, steaming for 10 to15 minutes. |

FUNKUO DUMPLINGS

❖ YIELD: 20 DUMPLINGS • PREPARATION: 30 MINUTES • COOKING: 5 TO 7 MINUTES ❖

¼ ounce (5 g) dried wood ear mushrooms
  (about a handful)
10½ ounces (300 g) pork filling
  (see recipe 23)

1 batch dumpling dough (see recipe 20)

1 2
3 4

1	Soak the wood ear mushrooms in cold water for 10 minutes.	2	Once the mushrooms are rehydrated, drain and coarsely chop them.	
3	Mix the mushrooms with the meat filling.	4	Roll out the dough and, with a cookie cutter, cut out 3-inch (8 cm) diameter circles.	➤

		CHICKEN VARIATION
5	Place a little filling in the middle of each circle and fold the pastry over the filling, forming a half moon. Lightly press the edges together to make them stick.	For the filling, you can substitute 1 pound (500 g) ground chicken for the ground pork loin. You can also add chopped green onions.

| 6 | Steam the dumplings in an oiled steamer basket for 5 to 7 minutes over high heat. | **STORAGE**
❋
These dumplings freeze well. To freeze, place them in a sealed container, separating each layer with plastic wrap. |

PEKING DUMPLINGS

❖ YIELD: ABOUT 40 DUMPLINGS • PREPARATION: 40 MINUTES • COOKING: 10 MINUTES ❖

3 Chinese or Napa cabbage leaves
1 pound (500 g) pork filling (see recipe 23)

FOR THE DOUGH:
2 cups (500 ml) flour
½ teaspoon (5 ml) salt
⅔ cup (150 ml) boiling water

TIP:
You can find prepared Chinese dumpling pastry circles in the freezer section of Asian supermarkets.

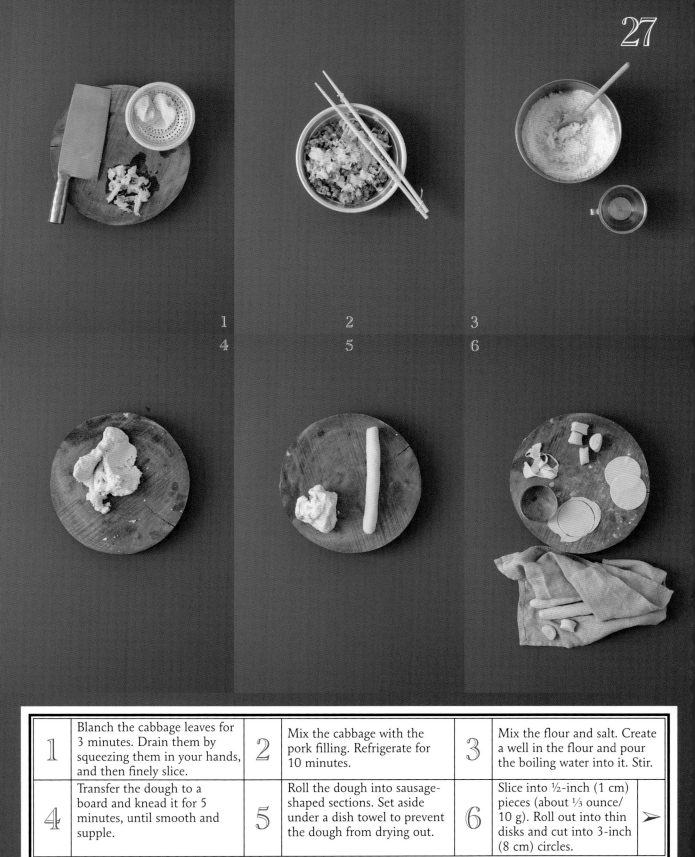

1	Blanch the cabbage leaves for 3 minutes. Drain them by squeezing them in your hands, and then finely slice.	2	Mix the cabbage with the pork filling. Refrigerate for 10 minutes.	3	Mix the flour and salt. Create a well in the flour and pour the boiling water into it. Stir.
4	Transfer the dough to a board and knead it for 5 minutes, until smooth and supple.	5	Roll the dough into sausage-shaped sections. Set aside under a dish towel to prevent the dough from drying out.	6	Slice into ½-inch (1 cm) pieces (about ⅓ ounce/ 10 g). Roll out into thin disks and cut into 3-inch (8 cm) circles. ➤

7 8
9 10

7	Place a little filling in the center of each circle.	8	Join the edges and make a pleat in the middle.
9	Continue sealing the dumpling by creating 3 pleats to the right then 3 pleats to the left, for a total of 7 pleats.	10	Arrange the dumplings in a steamer basket and steam for 8 to 10 minutes over high heat.

11	Serve the Peking dumplings hot with rice vinegar and finely sliced ginger.

TIP
❀

☞ The thinner the dough, the better tasting the dumplings will be.

COOKING OPTIONS
❀

Heat 1 tablespoon (15 ml) oil in a skillet. Line up the dumplings, fill halfway with water, and bring to a boil, covered. Cook until all the water has evaporated. Remove the cover and broil until the tops of the dumplings are golden.

DUCK & MUSHROOM DUMPLINGS

➤ YIELD: ABOUT 20 DUMPLINGS • PREPARATION: 25 MINUTES • COOKING: 15 MINUTES ➤

1 shallot
1 garlic clove
1 small bunch flat-leaf parsley
10½ ounces (300 g) white mushrooms

3 to 3½ ounces (80 to 100 g) smoked duck
  breast
2 tablespoons (30 ml) oil

2 tablespoons (30 ml) grated Parmesan
20 wonton skins
Salt & pepper, to taste

1 2
3 4

1	Chop the shallot, garlic and parsley. Clean the mushrooms and finely slice them.	2	Remove the fat from the smoked duck breast. Coarsely chop the duck meat.	
3	Lightly brown the shallot in the oil, and then add the mushrooms. Cook until golden.	4	Transfer the mushroom mixture to a bowl. Add the parsley, the Parmesan and the duck. Taste then season with salt and pepper, as desired.	➤

| 5 | Place a little filling on each wonton sheet. Moisten the edges with water and fold over to form rectangular dumplings. | **VARIATION**
※

You can substitute 2 confit duck thighs for the smoked duck breast. At step 3, remove the thigh flesh from the bones and brown it in duck fat along with the shallot. Follow the recipe method as described from step 4 onward. |

6	Oil a steamer basket or line the bottom of it with parchment paper. Arrange the dumplings in the basket and steam for 5 minutes.	**SERVING SUGGESTION** Serve with an arugula salad dressed with lemon juice and olive oil.

RICOTTA BITES

❖ YIELD: 25 BITES • PREPARATION: 20 MINUTES • COOKING: 5 MINUTES ❖

2 ounces (60 g) frozen spinach
8 roasted tomatoes
2 ounces (60 g) Parmesan
9 ounces (250 g) ricotta
  (about 1 cup/250 ml)

1 egg
Salt & pepper, to taste
25 wonton skins

PRELIMINARY:
Thaw the spinach then wring out any excess
water by squeezing firmly.

1

2

3

4

5

6

1	Chop the spinach and tomatoes. Grate the Parmesan.	2	Mix the cheeses, vegetables and egg, and season with salt and pepper.	3	Place a little filling in the center of the wonton skins.
4	Moisten the edges of each wonton. Fold the wonton over the filling to create a triangle. Press well to seal. Join the ends by sticking them together.	5	Arrange the bites in a steamer basket and steam for 5 minutes over high heat.	6	Serve the bites on their own or with a little pesto.

THAI MEATBALLS

✦ YIELD: 4 SERVINGS • PREPARATION: 30 MINUTES • COOKING: 8 MINUTES ✦

14 ounces (400 g) chicken breasts
3 kaffir lime leaves
1 stalk lemongrass
2 ounces (60 g) green beans
Salt, to taste

1 tablespoon (15 ml) red curry paste
  (or more, if desired)
1 egg
1 teaspoon (5 ml) sugar
2 tablespoons (30 ml) fish sauce

PRELIMINARY:
Chop the chicken breasts into chunks.

1 2
3 4

1	Mince the lime leaves. Remove the end of the lemongrass and the outside skin. Finely slice the lemongrass and the beans.	2	Place the chicken, 1 pinch salt, the curry paste, egg, sugar, fish sauce and lemongrass in a food processor or blender.	
3	Blend until you obtain a uniform and slightly sticky paste.	4	Transfer the mixture to a bowl, and add the lime leaves and green beans. Mix.	➢

	Dip your hands in a bowl of cold water and shape little chicken meatballs.	**TIP** ❉
5		☞ If you can't find kaffir lime leaves, you can use a piece of fresh ginger and lime zest instead.

		SERVING SUGGESTION
6	Place the chicken meatballs in a steamer basket and steam for 5 to 8 minutes over high heat. Serve with Thai Sauce (see recipe 1).	You can serve these meatballs, hot or cold, as an appetizer.

FISH BALLS

VARIATION OF THAI MEATBALLS

❋

Prepare these fish balls by following the method described in recipe 30. Substitute the same amount of cod for the chicken, and substitute green curry paste for the red curry paste. Shape the balls and steam for 5 to 8 minutes over high heat.

SURF & TURF MEATBALLS

VARIATION OF THAI MEATBALLS
❋

Blend 10½ ounces (300 g) chicken, 3½ ounces (100 g) squid or cuttlefish, 1 green onion (preferably a large and mature one) and 1 egg. Once the mixture is uniform, add some minced cilantro, the juice of ½ lime and a little salt and hot paprika. Shape the meatballs and steam for 5 to 8 minutes over high heat.

CHINESE BUN PASTRY

❧ YIELD: ABOUT 10 TO 12 BUNS • PREPARATION: 20 MINUTES • RESTING: 2 HOURS, 10 MINUTES ❧

FOR THE LEAVENING:
¼ ounce (7 g) yeast (about 1 teaspoon/5 ml)
½ cup + 1 tablespoon (140 ml) sugar
⅞ cup (200 ml) warm water
1⅔ cups (400 ml) flour

FOR THE DOUGH:
2½ cups (625 ml) flour
1 tablespoon (15 ml) baking powder
½ teaspoon (2 ml) baking soda
½ teaspoon (2 ml) salt

1 tablespoon (15 ml) vegetable oil
1 teaspoon (5 ml) white vinegar or lemon juice

1	Make the leavening first. Dilute the yeast and sugar in the water. Let rest for 10 minutes.	2	Mix in the flour and cover. Let rest for 1 hour in a warm place.	3	Heat the oven to 105°F (40°C). Using an electric mixer with a dough hook, mix all the ingredients for the dough. Add the leavening.
4	Knead in the mixer with the dough hook until the dough forms a uniform and smooth ball (about 10 minutes).	5	Oil a bowl, place the dough in the bowl and cover with plastic wrap.	6	Turn the oven off. Put the dough in the oven and leave for 1 hour. The dough must double in volume.

GLAZED PORK BUNS

✦ YIELD: 10 TO 12 BUNS • PREPARATION: 40 MINUTES • COOKING: 25 MINUTES • RESTING: 30 MINUTES ✦

1 tablespoon (15 ml) cornstarch
2 tablespoons (30 ml) soy sauce
2 tablespoons (30 ml) rice wine
1 tablespoon (15 ml) oyster sauce
1 tablespoon (15 ml) hoisin sauce

1 tablespoon (15 ml) sesame oil
⅓ cup (75 ml) water
1½ tablespoons (22 ml) sugar
1 pound (500 g) pork loin, coarsely diced
1 batch Chinese bun dough (see recipe 33)

PRELIMINARY:
Cut out 2-inch (5 cm) squares of parchment
paper. Dilute the cornstarch in a little water.

1 2
3 4

1	Place all the ingredients except the cornstarch and meat, in a saucepan. Cook for 5 minutes.	2	Add the meat. Stir and cook for 5 minutes.
3	Once the meat is fully cooked, add the cornstarch mixture.	4	Stir and cook until the sauce thickens, about 2 minutes. Let cool before using. The filling can be prepared up to 2 days in advance. ➤

5 6
7 8

5	Divide the dough into balls that weigh about 2½ ounces (70 g). Roll out the dough balls to form circles about 4 inches (10 cm) in diameter.	6	Place filling in the center of each dough circle, and fold over the edges, pleating and firmly pinching them to seal. Place each bun on a square of parchment paper.
7	Arrange the buns in a steamer basket. Cover with plastic wrap and let rise for 30 minutes.	8	Steam the buns over high heat for 15 minutes.

9	Serve immediately, in the basket if you wish. These buns can be served with spicy Sriracha sauce.

VARIATION
※

You can substitue the same amount of glazed pork (from a Chinese deli or supermarket) for the pork loin.

TIP
※

Chinese buns make a great snack. Just eat them with your hands — no cutlery!

STICKY RICE

❖ **YIELD: 4 SERVINGS** • PREPARATION: 5 MINUTES • COOKING: 20 MINUTES • RESTING: 3 HOURS OR OVERNIGHT ❖

2 cups (500 ml) uncooked sticky rice

PRELIMINARY:
Rinse the rice twice and let it soak in cold water for at least 3 hours, or overnight if possible.

1 2
3 4

1	Line the bottom of a steamer basket with a thin cloth dampened with water. Drain the rice and distribute it evenly inside the basket.	2	Bring a pot of water to a boil then place the basket overtop. Steam the rice for 10 minutes.
3	Fold the rice with a spatula. Cook for a further 5 to 10 minutes.	4	The rice is fully cooked when the grains are shiny. Taste test: if the rice is soft, it's cooked. Serve immediately as a side dish.

PORK SPARERIBS

➤ **YIELD: 4 SERVINGS** • PREPARATION: 10 MINUTES • MARINADING: 2 HOURS • COOKING: 30 MINUTES ➤

2 garlic cloves
2 small chili peppers (optional)
1 tablespoon (15 ml) fermented black beans
1 tablespoon (15 ml) oyster sauce
1 tablespoon (15 ml) soy sauce

1 tablespoon (15 ml) tapioca flour
1 tablespoon (15 ml) sugar
½ teaspoon (5 ml) salt
Black pepper, to taste

1¾ pounds (800 g) pork spareribs, defatted and cut into pieces (by a butcher)
1 small bunch cilantro

1 2
3 4

1	Chop the garlic, 1 chili pepper and the black beans.	2	Place the chopped garlic and beans, the whole chili pepper and the sauces, flour, sugar and salt in a bowl. Mix well and season with black pepper. Add the spareribs. Mix and let marinate for at least 2 hours, ideally overnight.
3	Place the spareribs in a deep dish and steam for 30 minutes over high heat.	4	When ready to serve, add the minced chili pepper and the cilantro sprigs. Serve with white rice.

GREEN ONION ROLLS

➤ YIELD: 4 SERVINGS • PREPARATION: 30 MINUTES • COOKING: 25 MINUTES ◄

9 ounces (250 g) frozen plums
1 star anise
½ ounce (15 g) fresh ginger, grated
2 cloves
2 heaping tablespoons (34 ml) brown sugar

2 heaping tablespoons (34 ml) rice wine vinegar
Salt, to taste
1 bunch green onions
1 pork tenderloin (about 1½ pounds/600 g)

3 tablespoons (45 ml) soy sauce
3 tablespoons (45 ml) sesame oil
Ground Japanese chili pepper (togarashi), to taste

1	Place the plums, anise, grated ginger, cloves and brown sugar in a saucepan. Add ¼ cup (60 ml) water. Let simmer over low heat for 20 minutes.	2	Once the sauce has thickened, remove the anise and the cloves.	
3	Blend with an immersion blender or in a stand blender and let cool. Taste and add the vinegar, salt and more brown sugar, as needed. The sauce should be bittersweet.	4	Wash the green onions and julienne them. Set aside.	➢

5 6
7 8

5	Slice the tenderloin into medallions. Flatten each medallion between 2 sheets of parchment paper to obtain a very thin slice of meat (like for carpaccio).	6	Spread a spoonful of plum sauce over each slice of tenderloin. Arrange julienned green onions on top.
7	Roll to form small rolls.	8	Place on a plate and steam for 5 minutes.

| 9 | Remove the rolls from the steamer basket. Top the rolls with soy sauce and sesame oil, and then sprinkle ground Japanese chili pepper on top. | **EXPRESS OPTIONS**
❋
You can buy prepared plum sauce in large supermarkets. You can also substitute leeks for the green onions and slices of prepared pork carpaccio for the pork tenderloin. Reduce the cooking time by half. |

TOFU WITH SOY SAUCE

❧ **YIELD: 2 SERVINGS** • **PREPARATION: 5 MINUTES** • **COOKING: 5 TO 7 MINUTES** ❧

3 green onions
1 block tofu
3 tablespoons (45 ml) soy sauce

2 tablespoons (30 ml) sesame oil
Ground Japanese chili pepper (togarashi),
   to taste

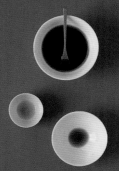

1 2
3 4

1	Wash and finely slice the green onions lengthwise.	2	Mix the soy sauce and sesame oil.
3	Place the tofu on a plate in a steamer basket and steam over medium heat for 5 to 7 minutes.	4	Remove the tofu and drain any water. Cut the tofu in half then slice it. Serve topped with the sauce, green onions and ground Japanese chili pepper.

CHAWANMUSHI

➤ YIELD: 6 SERVINGS • PREPARATION: 15 MINUTES • COOKING: 15 MINUTES ➤

6 dried shiitake mushrooms
9 ounces (250 g) chicken breast
4 tablespoons (60 ml) soy sauce
4 eggs
2½ cups (625 ml) dashi or chicken stock

1 small bunch shiso sprouts
Salt, to taste

PRELIMINARY:
Rehydrate the shiitake mushrooms in water.

TIP:
The right ratio is one part eggs to three parts stock. Crack the eggs into a measuring cup and note the volume. There should be 3 times that volume of stock.

1 2
3 4

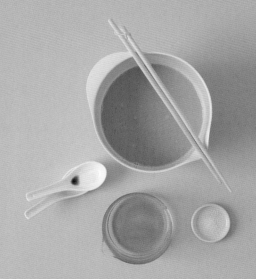

1	Chop the chicken and rehydrated shiitake mushrooms.	2	Season the chicken and shiitake mushrooms with 2 tablespoons (30 ml) soy sauce and a little salt. Set aside.
3	Crack the eggs into a measuring cup or bowl and fold with chopticks to mix. Do not whisk the eggs to prevent them from becoming foamy; they should have a silky texture.	4	Gradually add the stock and season with the remaining soy sauce and a little more salt. ➤

| 5 | Evenly distribute the chicken and mushrooms among six ramekins or bowls. Pour the stock mixture over the chicken and mushrooms, passing it through a strainer. Each ramekin should be about four-fifths full. | **VARIATION**
❊

Substitute shrimps for the chicken and celery heart leaves for the shiso sprouts. |

		TIP
6	Place the ramekins in a steamer basket, steam for 1 minute over high heat, and then lower the heat to minimum and steam for another 15 minutes. Check the doneness by pricking with a toothpick: if it comes out clean, the custard is ready. Finish by garnishing with the shiso sprouts.	You can prepare a family-sized chawanmushi in a large bowl. Cook for 18 to 20 minutes.

EASY VEGETABLES

HOME-STYLE VEGETABLES

ORIENTAL-STYLE VEGETABLES

LEEK VINAIGRETTE

➤ **YIELD: 4 SERVINGS** • PREPARATION: 15 MINUTES • COOKING: 15 MINUTES ◄

1 shallot
1 small bunch flat-leaf parsley
2 eggs
6 small leeks
½ teaspoon (2 ml) hot mustard

½ teaspoon (2 ml) whole-grain mustard
Salt & pepper, to taste
3 tablespoons (45 ml) red wine vinegar
4 tablespoons (60 ml) vegetable oil

PRELIMINARY:
Mince the shallot and the flat-leaf parsley.

1 2
3 4

1	Cook the eggs for 10 minutes. Peel and coarsely chop them. Set aside.	2	Wash the leeks and cut off and discard the ends. Steam the leeks in a steamer basket for 12 to 15 minutes, until tender.
3	Prepare the vinaigrette by mixing the mustards with the salt, pepper and vinegar. Whisk in the oil then add the shallot.	4	Sprinkle the vinaigrette, chopped egg and parsley on top of the leeks.

GREEN ASPARAGUS & FAVA BEANS

❖ **SERVES 4** • PREPARATION: 20 MINUTES • COOKING: 10 MINUTES ❖

14 ounces (400 g) frozen fava beans (broad beans) or 2¼ pounds (1 kg) unshelled fresh fava beans
3½ pounds (1.5 kg) green asparagus
1 bunch green onions, preferably large and mature

¼ cup (60 ml) balsamic vinegar
¼ cup (60 ml) olive oil
Salt & pepper, to taste

PRELIMINARY:
Boil the frozen fava beans in salted water for 2 minutes. If they are fresh, 1 minute will do.

1	Drain the fava beans then remove the skin, ensuring you do not split the beans. Set aside.	2	Remove and discard the ends from the green asparagus. Wash the asparagus.	3	Steam for 5 to 8 minutes in a steamer basket, until crisp-tender.
4	Wash and finely slice the green onions.	5	Whisk the vinegar and oil with a fork, and season with salt and pepper.	6	Arrange the asparagus on a platter, sprinkle the fava beans and the onions on top and then top with the sauce.

ASPARAGUS WITH HOLLANDAISE SAUCE

VARIATION ON GREEN ASPARAGUS & FAVA BEANS

Prepare a hollandaise sauce with ⅞ cup (210 ml) butter, 3 egg yolks and the juice of ½ lemon (see recipe 8). Wash and peel 3½ pounds (1.5 kg) white asparagus. Steam the asparagus in a steamer basket for about 10 to 15 minutes, depending on the size. Check the doneness of the asparagus by pricking with the tip of a knife: it must be tender. Serve hot, with the hollandaise sauce.

ASPARAGUS WITH MALTAISE SAUCE

VARIATION ON GREEN ASPARAGUS & FAVA BEANS
❖

Zest and juice 2 oranges. Heat the orange juice to reduce it by half. Prepare a maltaise sauce with ⅞ cup (210 ml) butter, 3 egg yolks, the juice of ½ lemon and the reduced orange juice (see recipe 10).

Wash and cut the ends of 3½ pounds (1.5 kg) green asparagus. Steam for about 10 minutes, depending on the size. The asparagus should be crisp-tender. Serve with the sauce and orange zest.

GREEN PEAS, MINT & RICOTTA

❧ **YIELD: 2 SERVINGS** • PREPARATION: 10 TO 20 MINUTES • COOKING: 7 MINUTES ❧

2¼ pounds (1 kg) fresh green peas or
   14 ounces (400 g) frozen
3 green onions

1 bunch mint
1 lemon
3 tablespoons (45 ml) olive oil

Salt & pepper, to taste
3½ ounces (100 g) ricotta, crumbled (about
   7 tablespoons/105 ml)

1 2
3 4

1	Shell the green peas.	2	Line the bottom of a steamer basket with parchment paper. Steam the green peas for 5 to 7 minutes.	
3	Wash and thinly slice the green onions. Pluck the mint leaves from the stems. Zest and juice the lemon.	4	Prepare a vinaigrette with half the lemon juice and the olive oil. Season with salt and pepper. Taste and adjust the seasoning as needed.	➢

5 | Remove the green peas from the steamer while they are still hot, and then add the green onions and vinaigrette. | **VARIATION**
❋
Substitute Parmesan shavings for the ricotta and basil for the mint. You can also add thin strips of Parma ham.

6 | Allow to cool before sprinkling crumbled ricotta, mint leaves and lemon zest on top.

SPRINGTIME VARIATION

❋

Mix the green peas with sugar snap peas and asparagus tips. Cook the sugar snap peas first for 2 minutes, and then add the green peas and asparagus tips.

ARTICHOKES WITH TWO SAUCES

⇥ YIELD: 2 SERVINGS • PREPARATION: 10 MINUTES • COOKING: 30 MINUTES ⇤

2 large artichokes
½ teaspoon (2 ml) whole-grain mustard
½ teaspoon (2 ml) hot mustard
2 tablespoons (30 ml) red wine vinegar
3 tablespoons (45 ml) vegetable oil

Salt & pepper, to taste
3 tablespoons (45 ml) crème fraîche or sour cream
1 small lemon, zested and juiced

PRELIMINARY:

Wash the artichokes by soaking in cold water for 5 minutes. Cut off and discard the stems.

1 2
3 4

1	Steam the artichokes in a steamer basket for 30 minutes (or cook for 10 minutes in a pressure cooker). Test doneness by pulling on a leaf: the artichokes are ready if the leaf is easy to remove.	2	Prepare a vinaigrette by mixing the two mustards and the vinegar, and then whisking in the oil. Season with salt and pepper.
3	Prepare the cream sauce by seasoning the crème fraîche with salt and pepper and adding the lemon zest and one quarter of the lemon juice. Taste and then adjust the seasoning, if necessary.	4	Serve the artichokes warm, with the two sauces.

CAULIFLOWER WITH CROUTONS

❖ **YIELD: 6 SERVINGS** • PREPARATION: 15 MINUTES • COOKING: 20 MINUTES ❖

5 ounces (150 g) slightly stale bread
  (about 4 or 5 slices)
1 small bunch flat-leaf parsley
1 large cauliflower

1 tablespoon (15 ml) oil
2½ tablespoons (37 ml) butter
Salt & pepper, to taste

PRELIMINARY:
Cut the bread to make small croutons.
Chop the flat-leaf parsley.

1 2
3 4

1	Cut the base off the cauliflower and discard. Wash the cauliflower and separate the florets. Cut any large florets in half lengthwise.	2	Steam the cauliflower florets in a steamer basket for 8 minutes.
3	Heat the oil then add the butter. Once the butter begins to foam, add the croutons and cook until golden.	4	Arrange the cauliflower in a dish, season with salt and pepper and sprinkle the croutons on top. Add the chopped parsley. Serve immediately.

STEAMED POTATOES

❖ **SERVES 4** • PREPARATION: 15 MINUTES • COOKING: 20 TO 30 MINUTES ❖

2 pounds (1 kg) firm potatoes
1 small bunch bay leaves
1 small bunch thyme
1 small bunch rosemary

FOR THE SAUCE:
1 small shallot
1 bunch chives
7 ounces (200 g) fromage blanc or queso blanco
Salt & ground pepper, to taste

PRELIMINARY:
Wash the potatoes.

1	Make a slit in a third of the potatoes and slide 1 bay leaf inside. Poke the rest of the potatoes with a skewer and insert 1 thyme sprig in half of them and 1 rosemary sprig in the other half.	2	Steam the potatoes in a steamer basket for 20 to 30 minutes, depending on the size. Prick using a knife to check doneness.
3	Meanwhile, mince the shallot and chives. Mix the herbs with the fromage blanc, and season with salt and pepper.	4	Serve the steamed potatoes hot, with the fromage blanc sauce and a little salt and pepper.

BUTTERED POTATOES

VARIATION OF STEAMED POTATOES

❋

Wash 2 pounds (1 kg) potatoes and steam for 20 to 30 minutes (per the method described in the preceding recipe, but omit the herbs) or cook in a pressure cooker for 10 minutes.

Serve the potatoes immediately with an assortment of flavored butters (see recipes 4, 5, 6 and 7).

POTATOES WITH WHIPPED CREAM

VARIATION OF STEAMED POTATOES

Wash and steam 2 pounds (1 kg) potatoes for 20 to 30 minutes. Mince a few sprigs of chives and dill, and then whip 1 cup (250 ml) heavy cream. Add ¼ cup (60 ml) lumpfish or salmon roe and the herbs, and then gently fold to mix. Taste and adjust the seasoning as needed. Serve the cooked potatoes with the whipped cream sauce.

MASHED POTATOES

❖ **SERVES 4** • PREPARATION: 15 MINUTES • COOKING: 30 MINUTES ❖

2 pounds (1 kg) potatoes
2 preserved lemons
7 tablespoons (105 ml) pine nuts

Olive oil, to taste
Salt & pepper, to taste

1 2
3 4

1	Wash and peel the potatoes. Slice any large ones in half. Dice the preserved lemons.	2	Place the potatoes in a steamer basket and arrange the diced lemon on top. Steam for 20 to 30 minutes.
3	Meanwhile, toast the pine nuts by heating them in a dry skillet over low heat until golden.	4	As soon as the potatoes are cooked, mash them with a fork, along with the preserved lemon. Generously drizzle olive oil on top of the potatoes. Season with salt and pepper, and serve with the pine nuts.

MASHED POTATOES WITH BEANS

VARIATION OF MASHED POTATOES
❋

Wash and peel 1½ pounds (600 g) potatoes, and steam with 1 garlic clove for 20 to 30 minutes. Cut the ends off 1 pound (500 g) green beans and place them in the second part of the steamer for 10 to 12 minutes. Once the potatoes are cooked, transfer to a dish. Peel the garlic clove, add the hot green beans and mash everything with a fork. Drizzle olive oil over top. Season with salt and pepper and serve.

MASHED SWEET POTATOES

VARIATION OF MASHED POTATOES
❋

Wash, peel and chop 2 pounds (1 kg) sweet potatoes. Steam for 20 to 25 minutes. Grate 1 ounce (20 g) fresh ginger and mince 4 to 5 cilantro sprigs. Once the potatoes are cooked, transfer to a dish and add 3 tablespoons (45 ml) butter, 1 teaspoon (5 ml) curry powder and the juice of ½ lime. Mash with a fork. Season with salt and pepper and sprinkle the minced cilantro on top.

ORIENTAL CARROTS

⇝ **SERVES 4 • PREPARATION: 15 MINUTES • COOKING: 20 MINUTES** ⇜

2¼ pounds (1 kg) carrots
3 garlic cloves
1 teaspoon (5 ml) cumin

1 tablespoon (15 ml) honey
1 small lemon, juiced
1 scant tablespoon (13 ml) harissa

3 tablespoons (45 ml) olive oil
Salt & pepper, to taste
½ bunch cilantro, minced

1 2
3 4

1	Wash, peel and slice the carrots into thick rounds.	2	Steam the carrot rounds and garlic cloves in a steamer basket for 10 minutes. Remove the garlic cloves and steam the carrots for an additional 10 minutes.
3	Meanwhile, prepare a vinaigrette by mixing the cumin, the honey, half the lemon juice, the harissa and the oil. Season with salt and pepper.	4	Crush the steamed garlic and mix into the vinaigrette. ➤

| 5 | Once the carrots are cooked, top with the vinaigrette and mix well. Taste then adjust the seasoning if necessary. | **VARIATION**
❋
Steam 2 pounds (1 kg) potatoes then peel and dice them. Prepare a vinaigrette using the juice from half a lemon, a little salt, 3 tablespoons (45 ml) olive oil and 1 heaping tablespoon (17 ml) harissa. Top the warm potatoes with the vinaigrette. Serve cold. |

		SERVING SUGGESTION
	Serve warm or cold, topped with minced cilantro.	❋
6		Serve these carrots with steamed fish.

ZUCCHINI & FAVA BEANS WITH CUMIN

⇥ **SERVES 4** • PREPARATION: 20 MINUTES • COOKING: 10 MINUTES ⇤

3 zucchini
9 ounces (250 g) fresh or frozen fava beans
   (broad beans), shelled

1 teaspoon (5 ml) ground cumin
1 small lemon, juiced
3 tablespoons (45 ml) olive oil

Salt & pepper, to taste
1 small bunch cilantro

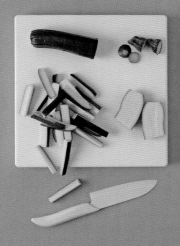

1   2   3

4   5   6

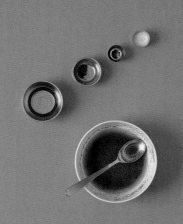

1	Wash the zucchini, and then quarter and slice into 2-inch (5 cm) long sections.	2	Steam in a steamer basket for 8 to 10 minutes.	3	Boil the beans for 1 minute (if using frozen beans boil for 2 to 3 minutes).
4	Drain the beans then peel off the skins.	5	Whisk together the cumin, half of the lemon juice, the oil, the salt and the pepper.	6	Mix the steamed zucchini, the beans and the cumin vinaigrette. Sprinkle cilantro on top and serve warm.

EGGPLANT WITH SESAME

➤ **SERVES 4** • **PREPARATION: 15 MINUTES** • **COOKING: 20 MINUTES** ➤

1 small bunch cilantro
3 green onions
1 garlic clove
3 eggplants (about 2 pounds/900 g)

1 tablespoon (15 ml) sesame seeds
1 teaspon (5 ml) sugar
½ lemon, juiced
2 tablespoons (30 ml) tahini (sesame paste)

1 tablespoon (15 ml) sesame oil
2 tablespoons (30 ml) soy sauce
Salt, to taste
1 red chili pepper (optional)

1 2
3 4

1	Wash the cilantro and green onions. Pluck the cilantro leaves from the stems, and finely slice the green onions. Chop the garlic clove.	2	Wash and slice the eggplants into chunks.	
3	Steam the eggplant in a steamer basket until tender, about 15 to 20 minutes. Remove from the heat and set aside.	4	Toast the sesame seeds in a dry skillet, stirring often. Remove from the heat when golden.	➤

5

Mix the sugar into the lemon juice. Next, mix in the tahini, sesame oil, soy sauce, chopped garlic and salt.

		VARIATION
		❋
6	Top the eggplant with the dressing. Taste and adjust the seasoning, if needed. Serve cold, topped with the cilantro, green onion and chili pepper, if using.	You can substitute peanut butter for the tahini. Dilute the sauce with a little using water if it's too thick.

BOK CHOY IN OYSTER SAUCE

SERVES 4 • PREPARATION: 10 MINUTES • COOKING: 5 MINUTES

6 small or 4 large bok choy cabbages
2 tablespoons (30 ml) oyster sauce

3 tablespoons (45 ml) garlic oil (see recipe 2)
Salt, to taste

1 2
3 4

1	Wash the bok choy. Slice in half or quarters lengthwise, depending on the size.	2	Steam the bok choy in a steamer basket for 3 to 5 minutes.
3	Mix the oyster sauce and garlic oil. Season with salt.	4	Place the cooked bok choy in a dish, top with the sauce and mix. Serve immediately.

NAPA CABBAGE IN OYSTER SAUCE

VARIATION OF BOK CHOY IN OYSTER SAUCE

❋

Wash the Napa cabbage and slice into sixths or eighths lengthwise, depending on the size. Steam in a steamer basket for 3 to 5 minutes. Mix 2 tablespoons (30 ml) oyster sauce and 3 tablespoons (45 ml) garlic oil (see recipe 2). Season with salt. Place the cooked cabbage in a dish, top with sauce and mix. Serve immediately.

BROCCOLI IN OYSTER SAUCE

VARIATION OF BOK CHOY IN OYSTER SAUCE
❋

Separate the florets of 1¾ pounds (800 g) broccoli, and slice the largest ones in half. Steam for 5 to 10 minutes. Mix 2 tablespoons (30 ml) oyster sauce and 3 tablespoons (45 ml) garlic oil (see recipe 2). Season with salt. Top with the sauce, mix and serve.

MUSHROOMS WITH GINGER

❧ SERVES 4 • PREPARATION: 20 MINUTES • COOKING: 6 MINUTES ❧

1¾ pounds (800 g) assorted Asian
  mushrooms (dried shiitakes, king
  or regular oyster mushrooms, enoki
  and/or buna-shimeji)
1 small bunch green onions

3 garlic cloves
2 ounces (60 g) fresh ginger
4 tablespoons (60 ml) oil
2 tablespoons (30 ml) oyster sauce
Salt & pepper, to taste

PRELIMINARY:
Remove and discard any woody stems from
the mushrooms.

1 2
3 4

1	Soak any dried mushrooms in cold water until completely rehydrated (about 15 minutes).	2	Clean the rest of the mushrooms using a damp paper towel. Chop the large mushrooms into chunks.
3	Wash the green onions. Cut the white part in half or in quarters. Finely slice the green part. Set both parts aside.	4	Peel the garlic cloves and ginger. Slice the garlic and julienne the ginger. Set aside. ➢

5 6
7 8

5	Arrange the larger mushrooms and the white parts of the green onions in a steamer basket. Steam for 5 minutes.	6	Meanwhile, lightly brown the ginger and garlic in the oil. Cook until the garlic slices are golden. Set aside.
7	After the mushrooms have been steaming for 5 minutes, add the smaller mushrooms (buna-shimeji and enoki). Steam for an additional minute.	8	Once the mushrooms are cooked, transfer to a bowl. Add the garlic-ginger oil and the oyster sauce. Season with salt and pepper.

		SERVING SUGGESTION
9	Top with the finely sliced spring onions and serve immediately.	Serve with white rice or noodles.

PAPILLOTES & STUFFED DISHES

4

PAPILLOTES

ROLLS AND OTHER FILLED DISHES

SALMON & SPINACH EN PAPILLOTE

❖ **YIELD: 2 SERVINGS** • PREPARATION: 5 MINUTES • COOKING: 12 MINUTES ❖

1 small shallot
5 ounces (150 g) baby spinach
2 heaping tablespoons (34 ml) sour cream
Salt & pepper, to taste

Nutmeg, to taste
2 salmon fillets of about 7 ounces
   (200 g) each

PRELIMINARY:
Mince the shallot.

1 2
3 4

1	Evenly distribute the baby spinach, shallot and sour cream on 2 sheets of parchment paper. Season with salt, pepper and grated nutmeg.	2	Arrange the salmon fillets on top. Season again.
3	Fold the edges of the parchment paper over the salmon and tie with twine.	4	Steam for 10 to 12 minutes. To avoid over-steaming the fish, finish cooking the papillotes in a microwave oven for a few seconds, if needed.

COD & SUGAR SNAP PEAS EN PAPILLOTE

❧ **YIELD: 2 SERVINGS** • **PREPARATION: 20 MINUTES** • **COOKING: 5 TO 10 MINUTES** ❧

9 ounces (250 g) sugar snap peas
2 cod fillets of about 7 to 9 ounces (200 to
   250 g) each
Salt & pepper, to taste

¼ cup (60 ml) tomato-basil butter (see
   recipe 7)

PRELIMINARY:
Boil the sugar snap peas in salted water for
2 minutes if you don't want them to be too
crunchy.

1 2
3 4

1	Debone the fish fillets.	2	Evenly distribute the peas and cod on two sheets of parchment paper. Season with salt and pepper. Add pieces of tomato-basil butter.
3	Seal the papillotes by joining the edges, folding over and pressing firmly. Seal the ends and fold over to avoid any leaks.	4	Steam in a steamer basket for 5 to 10 minutes over high heat. If necessary, finish cooking in a microwave oven for a few seconds.

SEA BREAM & FENNEL EN PAPILLOTE

↠ YIELD: 2 SERVINGS • PREPARATION: 10 MINUTES • COOKING: 5 TO 10 MINUTES ↞

2 sea bream fillets
1 fennel bulb
Salt & pepper, to taste

3 tablespoons (45 ml) almond-lemon butter
(see recipe 6)
1 small lemon, cut into wedgess

1 2
3 4

1	Debone the fish.	2	Slice the fennel using a vegetable peeler or mandoline.
3	Evenly distribute the fennel on 2 sheets of parchment paper. Season with salt and pepper. Add the sea bream, season again and sprinkle pieces of almond-citrus butter on top.	4	Seal the papillotes and steam in a steaming basket for 5 to 10 minutes, depending on the thickness of the sea bream fillets. Serve immediately, with lemon wedges.

RED MULLET À LA NIÇOISE

❧ **YIELD: 4 SERVINGS** • **PREPARATION: 30 MINUTES** • **COOKING: 12 MINUTES** ❧

12 red mullet fillets
Salt and pepper to taste
¼ cup (60 ml) niçoise olives
1 bunch fresh basil

FOR THE TOMATO CONCASSÉ:
1 pound (500 g) tomatoes
1 small onion
2 garlic cloves
3 tablespoons olive oil

1 bouquet garni (1 bay leaf and 1 sprig
  thyme tied with string)
Salt & pepper, to taste
1 teaspoon (5 ml) sugar

1 2
3 4

1	Remove and discard the stems from the tomatoes. Score the tomatoes with the tip of a knife.	2	Plunge the tomatoes in boiling water for 1 to 2 minutes. Let them cool for a few seconds then peel off the skins.	
3	Seed then dice the tomatoes.	4	Mince the onion and chop the garlic.	➤

5 6
7 8

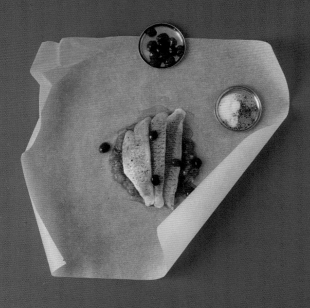

5	Sweat the onion in the olive oil, and then add the tomatoes, garlic and bouquet garni. Season with salt and pepper and add the sugar.	6	Place a perforated disk of parchment paper directly on top of the tomatoes. Cook over low heat for 20 minutes.
7	Evenly distribute the tomato concassé on 4 sheets of parchment paper. Place 3 red mullet fillets on top of each, and season with salt and pepper. Sprinkle the olives on top.	8	Seal the papillotes and steam for 5 minutes in a steamer basket.

9	Open the papillotes and add a few basil leaves. Serve immediately with a drizzle of olive oil, if desired.	☛ If you're pressed for time, you can substitute canned stewed tomatoes for the tomato concassé. Heat the tomatoes in a microwave oven before distributing onto the parchment paper.

MUSSELS WITH LEMONGRASS

➤ **YIELD: 4 SERVINGS** • **PREPARATION: 20 MINUTES** • **SOAKING: 15 MINUTES** • **COOKING: 10 MINUTES** ➤

1 small bunch Thai basil
3 stalks lemongrass
2 pounds (1 kg) mussels
1 small onion
1 small piece of galangal or ginger
3 garlic cloves

1 red chili pepper (optional)
3 tablespoons (45 ml) vegetable oil
1 teaspoon (5 ml) sugar
2 tablespoons (30 ml) fish sauce
½ lime, juiced

PRELIMINARY:

Wash the basil and pick the leaves off the stems. Remove the outside leaves from the lemongrass stalks.

1 2
3 4

1	De-beard the mussels (i.e., remove any tough, stringy filaments). Rinse under running water then soak in cold water for 15 minutes, to remove any impurities.	2	Finely slice the lemongrass, onion and galangal. Chop the garlic and chili pepper, if using.
3	Heat the oil in a skillet. Lightly brown the onion along with the garlic, galangal, lemongrass and chili pepper.	4	After 2 to 3 minutes, add the sugar, fish sauce and lime juice. Remove from the heat. ➢

5	Evenly distribute the mussels on 4 sheets of parchment paper. Top with the lemongrass mixture. Sprinkle basil on top.	**SPICY VARIATION** ❋ Add 1 tablespoon (15 ml) red curry paste to the onions with browning. Thin the sauce with a little water or coconut milk.	

6	Fold over the edges of the paper to form a package and tie with twine. Steam for 5 to 10 minutes. Serve immediately.	**VARIATION** ❋	This recipe works well with all kinds of shellfish: cockles, quahogs, clams, razor clams, etc.

CHICKEN WITH WHITE WINE EN PAPILLOTE

❖ YIELD: 2 SERVINGS • PREPARATION: 20 MINUTES • COOKING: 10 TO 15 MINUTES ❖

2 garlic cloves
2 chicken breasts
3½ ounces (100 g) assorted dried
  mushrooms or 9 ounces (250 g) fresh
  mushrooms

Salt & pepper, to taste
2 to 4 sprigs thyme
7 tablespoons (105 ml) white wine
2½ tablespoons (37 ml) butter

PRELIMINARY:
Slice the garlic and the cut the chicken into
chunks.

1 2
3 4

1	Soak dried mushrooms in warm water. If using fresh mushrooms, remove and discard any woody stems, then wash and slice the mushrooms in half or in quarters.	2	Season the chicken with salt and pepper, and, in a bowl, mix with the garlic, thyme and white wine. Let marinate for 10 minutes, or until the mushrooms are completely rehydrated.
3	Evenly distribute the mushrooms on 2 sheets of parchment paper. Season with salt and pepper. Evenly distribute the pieces of chicken on the paper, pour a little marinade over and top with knobs of butter.	4	Seal the papillote by folding over the edges and tie with twine. Steam for 10 to 15 minutes. You can add 1 tablespoon (15 ml) sour cream to each papillote before sealing.

CHINESE CHICKEN EN PAPILLOTE

VARIATION OF CHICKEN WITH WHITE WINE EN PAPILLOTE
❋

Rehydrate a handful of wood ear mushrooms and 6 shiitake mushrooms, and thinly slice once rehydrated. Thinly slice 10½ ounces (300 g) of chicken breast. Marinate the chicken for 10 minutes with 3 tablespoons (45 ml) soy sauce, 1 tablespoon (15ml) oyster sauce, 2 tablespoons (30 ml) garlic oil (see recipe 2) and 1 teaspoon (5 ml) sugar.

Season with salt and pepper. Evenly distribute the chicken on 2 squares of parchment paper, and add 5 ounces (150 g) bamboo shoots and the mushrooms. Seal the papillotes. Steam for 15 minutes. Top with thinly sliced green onions.

COCONUT CHICKEN EN PAPILLOTE

VARIATION OF CHICKEN WITH WHITE WINE EN PAPILLOTE

✳

Coarsely chop 10½ ounces (300 g) chicken breast. Thinly slice 2 stalks lemongrass. Mince 4 to 5 kaffir lime leaves. Marinate the chicken for 10 minutes in the zest and juice of ½ lime, 2 tablespoons (30 ml) fish sauce, 1 cup (250 ml) coconut milk, 1 teaspoon (5 ml) sugar, the lemongrass and the lime leaves. Evenly distribute 7 ounces (200 g) sugar snap peas (boiled for 2 minutes) and the chicken on 2 squares of parchment paper. Top with a little marinade. Seal. Steam for 10 to 15 minutes. Garnish with cilantro and fresh red chili pepper.

SOLE ROLLS

❧ **YIELD: 2 SERVINGS** • **PREPARATION: 20 MINUTES** • **COOKING: 10 MINUTES** ❧

3½ ounces (100 g) gray shrimp
1 small bunch chives
1 small shallot

5½ tablespoons (82 ml) almond-lemon butter (see recipe 6), softened (or more if you will be serving with steamed potatoes [see recipe 47])

4 sole fillets
Salt & pepper, to taste

1   2   3

4   5   6

1	Shell the shrimp and coarsely chop them.	2	Mince the chives and shallot.	3	Mix the shrimps, chives and shallot into the softened butter.
4	Lightly flatten the sole fillets between 2 sheets of parchment paper.	5	Season the fillets with salt and pepper and top with 1 large spoonful of shrimp butter. Roll into a tight package.	6	Place the rolls on a plate and steam for 8 to 10 minutes. Serve immediately.

SALMON BUNDLES

❧ **YIELD: 2 SERVINGS** • **PREPARATION: 15 MINUTES** • **COOKING: 10 MINUTES** ❧

1 small shallot
7 ounces (200 g) whiting or cod fillets
1 egg white
7 tablespoons (105 ml) heavy cream (36%)
8½ ounces (240 g) marinated or fresh
    salmon carpaccio (about 8 to 10 slices)

Salt & pepper, to taste

PRELIMINARY:
Peel and mince the shallot. Debone the fish fillets.

TIPS:
You can add a mixture of diced mixed vegetables, herbs or spinach to the filling.

1 2
3 4

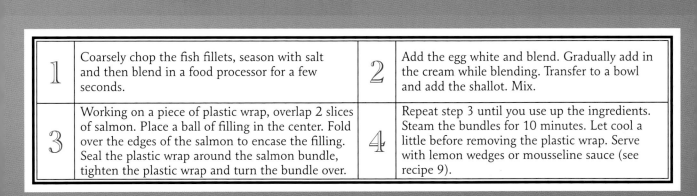

1	Coarsely chop the fish fillets, season with salt and then blend in a food processor for a few seconds.	2	Add the egg white and blend. Gradually add in the cream while blending. Transfer to a bowl and add the shallot. Mix.
3	Working on a piece of plastic wrap, overlap 2 slices of salmon. Place a ball of filling in the center. Fold over the edges of the salmon to encase the filling. Seal the plastic wrap around the salmon bundle, tighten the plastic wrap and turn the bundle over.	4	Repeat step 3 until you use up the ingredients. Steam the bundles for 10 minutes. Let cool a little before removing the plastic wrap. Serve with lemon wedges or mousseline sauce (see recipe 9).

GUINEA FOWL BALLOTINE

⬧ YIELD: 4 TO 6 SERVINGS • PREPARATION: 50 MINUTES • COOKING: 40 MINUTES ⬧

1 large caul (available from a butcher)
2 shallots
1 small bunch flat-leaf parsley
1 garlic clove
1 pound (500 g) white mushrooms

5 ounces (150 g) bacon
¼ cup (60 ml) vegetable oil
Salt & pepper, to taste
1 tablespoon (15 ml) port (optional)
2 tablespoons (30 ml) grated Parmesan

¾ cup (175 ml) bread crumbs
1 guinea fowl, deboned by a butcher
2 teaspoons (10 ml) butter (optional)

1	Soak the caul in cold water to remove any impurities. Set aside.	2	Mince the shallots and the parsley, chop the garlic and dice the mushrooms and bacon.
3	Sweat the shallots in half of the oil, and add the bacon and mushrooms. Season with salt and pepper. Brown until golden.

| 4 | Remove from the heat, and add the parsley, garlic, port and grated Parmesan. Mix in the bread crumbs. | 5 | Put the guinea fowl, fleshy side up, on a flat work surface. Season with salt and pepper. Spread the mushroom mixture on top and roll up the guinea fowl. | 6 | Wring the caul to remove any excess water, spread it out and place the guinea fowl on top. | ➤ |

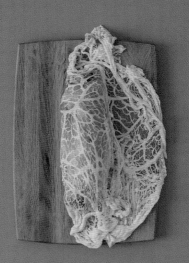

7 8
9 10

7	Completely wrap the guinea fowl in the caul.	8	Fold over the ends toward the bottom, and tie with twine to hold everything together.
9	Steam the ballotine in a steamer basket for 30 to 40 minutes. Let cool.	10	In a skillet, heat the remaining oil with the butter. Brown the ballotine on all sides.

| 11 | Slice and serve immediately. The ballotine can be accompanied by a mesclun salad dressed with balsamic vinegar and olive oil. You can also serve it with a mixture of steamed vegetables. | **TIP**
❋
You can substitute plastic wrap for the caul. Make small holes in the plastic wrap before steaming the ballotine. |

CHICKEN MAKI ROLLS

❖ YIELD: 2 SERVINGS • PREPARATION: 20 MINUTES • COOKING: 15 MINUTES ❖

1 shallot
8 ounces (225 g) cream cheese or other soft
  white cheese (about 1 cup/250 ml)

Salt & pepper, to taste
1 large zucchini
14 ounces (400 g) chicken breast

½ bunch basil
1 cup (250 ml) roasted tomatoes

1 2
3 4

1	Mince the shallot.	2	Mix the shallot with the cheese. Season with salt and pepper.	
3	Slice the zucchini lengthwise using a vegetable peeler or mandoline.	4	Butterfly the chicken breasts by slicing into each side and opening then up like a wallet.	➤

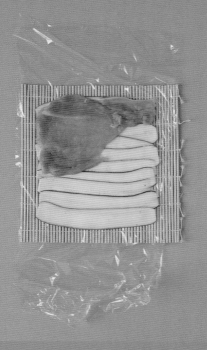

5 6
7 8

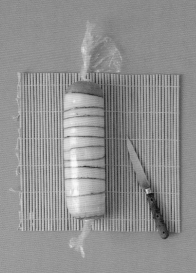

5	Overlap slices of zucchini on a bamboo sushi mat covered with plastic wrap. Top with slices of chicken. Season with salt and pepper.	6	Spread the cheese mixture on the chicken. Arrange a row of basil leaves and a row of roasted tomatoes on top.
7	Roll up using the plastic wrap and the bamboo mat. Tightly seal the wrap around the roll and twist the ends. Create small holes in the plastic wrap using the tip of a knife.	8	Steam for 10 to 15 minutes.

| 9 | Let the roll cool completely before slicing into small, sushi-like rolls. This dish is ideal for a cold buffet or a picnic. | **SERVING SUGGESTION**
❈
Serve chicken maki with a mesclun salad or a pasta salad. |

RABBIT WITH DRIED FRUIT

➤ YIELD: 4 SERVINGS • PREPARATION: 45 MINUTES • COOKING: 20 MINUTES ➤

3 dried figs	10½ ounces (300 g) bacon	½ teaspoon (2 ml) cinnamon
6 dried apricots	Salt & pepper, to taste	2 tablespoons (30 ml) honey
5 prunes	2 onions	½ cup (125 ml) white wine
2 to 3 rabbit saddles	1 tablespoon (15 ml) vegetable oil	

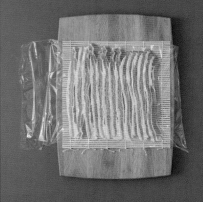

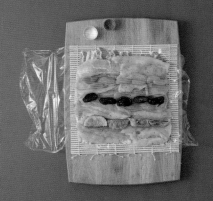

1	Coarsely chop the dried fruit.	2	Slice the rabbit saddles lengthwise, to make small cutlets.	3	Lay plastic wrap on a bamboo sushi mat. Overlap the bacon slices on the plastic wrap.	
4	Place the rabbit saddles on the bacon and season with salt and pepper. Arrange rows of dried fruit on top.	5	Roll tightly using the bamboo mat and plastic wrap. Tighten and twist the ends of the plastic wrap around the rabbit ballotine.	6	Steam in a steamer basket for 15 minutes.	➤

7 8
9 10

7	Meanwhile, thinly slice the onions.	8	Brown the onions in the oil. When golden, add the cinnamon, honey and the remaining dried fruit. Let caramelize. Set aside.
9	Remove the plastic wrap from around the rabbit ballotine and brown it on all sides in the oil. Set aside and keep warm.	10	Deglaze the skillet with the white wine. Return the onion and the dried-fruit mixture to the pan. Season then let stew. Taste and adjust the seasoning, if necessary.

11 Slice the rabbit ballotine and serve with the onion and dried-fruit compote.	**TECHNIQUE** ❊ The bamboo mat and plastic wrap will help you to shape the ballotine. After each turn, unstick the mat and wrap from the ballotine and reset to start a new turn. Take care not to roll the plastic wrap into the ballotine. The plastic wrap only serves to cover the ballotine and hold it together during cooking.

SERVING SUGGESTION
❊

This dish can be served with a salad or couscous.

STUFFED CABBAGE LEAVES

❧ YIELD: 6 SERVINGS • PREPARATION: 40 MINUTES • COOKING: 15 MINUTES ❧

1 garlic clove
1 sprig rosemary
1 small savoy cabbage
2 ounces (60 g) slightly stale bread (about
  1 or 2 slices)

⅔ cup (150 ml) milk
14 ounces (400 g) fresh sausage
1 sprig thyme
¼ cup (60 ml) Parmesan
Salt & pepper, to taste

PRELIMINARY:
Chop the garlic. Pluck the rosemary leaves
from the stems and chop them.

1	Remove the cabbage leaves from the head, taking care not to rip them. Plunge them in boiling water for 5 minutes, just enough time to soften them. Drain and set aside.	2	Soak the bread in the milk.	
3	Remove the casing from the sausage, and break the meat apart with a fork.	4	Wring any excess milk from the bread. Mix the bread with the sausage meat. Add the garlic, thyme, rosemary and grated Parmesan. Season with salt and pepper.	➤

		TYING THE CABBAGE LEAVES
5	Remove the tough center vein from the middle of each cabbage leaf. Place a little ball of filling in the center of each leaf, fold over to seal the filling and tie with kitchen twine to create little bundles.	Place the cabbage-leaf bundle on a piece of twine. Make the first knot. Cross the twine over the bundle, turn the bundle over and make another knot.

	Steam the bundles in a steamer basket for 10 to 15 minutes. Serve hot with rice and some tomato concassé (see recipe 63).	**TIP** ❋ You can prepare the cabbage bundles a day in advance and reheat them in a small saucepan with a little olive oil and water.
6		

MUSHROOM CABBAGE ROLLS

VARIATION OF STUFFED CABBAGE LEAVES
❋

Prepare a mushroom filling as described in recipe 70. Briefly boil the leaves of 1 savoy cabbage as explained in recipe 73.

Place a tablespoon of filling on each leaf, fold the sides in and roll tightly. Drizzle a little oil on top and steam for 15 to 20 minutes.

NAPA CABBAGE ROLLS

VARIATION OF STUFFED CABBAGE LEAVES

❋

Boil the leaves of 1 small Napa or Chinese cabbage for 3 minutes. Drain and remove the base of the leaves. Place a little meat filling (see recipe 23) on each leaf, fold the edges in and roll tightly, like a cigar. Steam for 10 minutes. Remove from the heat and top with soy sauce and sesame oil or garlic oil (see recipe 2).

SPECIAL
SUPPERS

VEGETABLES

FISH & SEAFOOD

MEAT & POULTRY

PARTY DIPS

➤ **YIELD: 8 SERVINGS (AS AN APPETIZER) • PREPARATION: 40 MINUTES • COOKING: 15 TO 20 MINUTES** ➤

3 little gem lettuces
1 celery heart
1 bunch radishes
1 small cauliflower
1 bunch carrots with tops
2 zucchini

1 cucumber
2 small fennels bulbs
1 pound (500 g) fingerling potatoes
1 bunch baby artichokes
12 quail eggs
1 lemon, cut into wedges

1 batch aioli (see recipe 14)
1 batch tapenade (see recipe 16)
1 batch anchovy paste (see recipe 15)
PRELIMINARY: Wash all the vegetables. Slice the lettuces into segments and separate the ribs of the celery heart.

1 2
3 4

1	Boil the quail eggs until fully cooked (hard yolks). Let them cool then peel off the shells. Set aside.	2	Wash the radishes, cut off any little roots and remove any dead leaves.
3	Separate the florets of the cauliflower.	4	Peel the carrots and cut into thick strips. ➤

5 6
7 8

5	Cut the zucchini and cucumber into strips about the same size as the carrots.	6	Cut the fennel bulbs into wedges.
7	Place the fingerling potatoes, half the carrots, half the fennel, the cauliflower and the zucchini in a steamer basket. Steam for 10 minutes over high heat, until crisp-tender. Remove most of the vegetables, leaving only the potatoes. Continue steaming the potatoes until cooked through.	8	Cut the stems off the baby artichokes, and remove and discard the outside dead leaves. Cut the artichokes into quarters lengthwise and set aside in water with lemon.

9   Slice the quail eggs in half. Arrange the cooked vegetables, the raw vegetables and the quail eggs halves on a large platter. Serve with the different sauces.

TIP
❋

For a dish that is even more complete, add pieces of roast chicken or cooked shrimp.

MORE DIPS
❋

For even greater variety, add guacamole (see recipe 77), light tartar sauce (see recipe 17) and tzatziki (see recipe 18).

STEAMED CRAB

➤ YIELD: 2 SERVINGS • PREPARATION: 15 MINUTES • COOKING: 25 TO 30 MINUTES ➤

2 large crabs, preferably female
1 batch Thai sauce (see recipe 1)
FOR THE GUACAMOLE:
2 tomatoes
½ onion
1 small bunch cilantro

1 red chili pepper
2 avocadoes
1 lime
Salt & pepper, to taste
FOR THE TARTAR SAUCE:
2 hard-boiled eggs

1 small bunch each chervil, flat-leaf parsley
 & chives
1 batch mayonnaise (see recipe 11)
PRELIMINARY:
Place the crabs in the freezer so they fall
asleep.

1

2

3

4

5

6

1	To prepare the guacamole, dice the tomatoes. Mince the onion and cilantro. Chop the red chili pepper.	2	Mash the flesh of the avocadoes with a fork, and mix with the juice of half a lime.	3	Add the tomato, onion, cilantro and chili pepper to the avocado. Season with salt and pepper. Taste and adjust the seasoning with lime juice.
4	To prepare the tartar sauce, chop the hard-boiled eggs and finely chop the herbs.	5	Mix the herbs and eggs with the mayonnaise. Set aside.	6	Steam the crabs for about 25 to 30 minutes. ➢

| 7 | Separate the crabs' pincers and legs from their bodies. Insert a knife into the back of the crab, between the shell and the body. Pull toward you to open up the body. Remove the gills. If desired, place the hepatopancreas, commonly called the "mustard," in a bowl. Slice the body in half or in quarters. Snap the pincers and legs to open. | **TIP** ❋

 Fresh crab is available year round. Summer is the best time of year to enjoy it in colder climates, but those who live close the warm waters will find crab is plentiful during the winter. |

		OPTION
8	Let cool before serving with the sauces.	You can substitute spider crabs or jumbo shrimps for the crabs. Cook them whole for between 4 and 8 minutes, depending on the size.

SHRIMPS WITH TOMATO BUTTER

⇒ YIELD: 3 SERVINGS • PREPARATION: 20 MINUTES • COOKING: 5 MINUTES **⇐**

12 jumbo shrimps

FOR THE TOMATO-BASIL BUTTER:
1 bunch basil
1¾ ounces (50 g) roasted tomatoes
1 cup (250 ml) butter, softened

⅓ cup (75 ml) grated Parmesan
1 teaspoon (5 ml) whole-grain mustard
1 teaspoon (5 ml) hot paprika

1 2
3 4

1	Coarsely chop the basil, and slice the tomatoes.	2	Place all the ingredients for the tomato-basil butter in a bowl.
3	Mix well, until the flavorings are uniformly distributed in the butter. Set aside at room temperature.	4	Split the shrimps lengthwise. ➢

| 5 | Place pieces of butter on each shrimp half. | **TIP** ❁ |
| | | You can find large and jumbo frozen shrimps in large supermarkets and in Asian supermarkets. |

6	Place the dressed shrimps in a steamer basket and steam for barely 5 minutes.	**VARIATION** ❋
		In season, substitute fresh langoustines for the shrimps.

SCALLOPS WITH LEEK CREAM

⇢ YIELD: 2 SERVINGS • PREPARATION: 20 MINUTES • COOKING: 20 MINUTES ⇠

1 shallot
2 teaspoons (10 ml) butter
2 small leeks

⅔ cup (150 ml) dry vermouth or dry white
   wine
⅔ cup (150 ml) crème fraîche or sour cream

Salt & pepper, to taste
8 large scallops

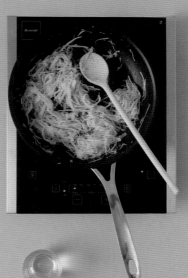

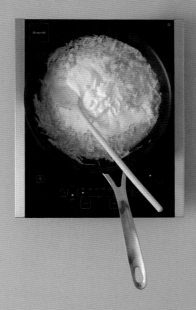

1	Mince the shallot and julienne the leek (cut into strips).	2	Sweat the shallot in the butter. Add the leeks and cook for 2 minutes. Pour in the vermouth and reduce; the liquid must be absorbed.
3	Next, add in the crème fraîche and reduce by half. Season with salt and pepper. Set aside and keep warm.	4	Steam the scallops for 2 to 3 minutes in a steamer basket. Distribute the leek cream on each plate. Place the scallops on top. Season with salt and pepper and serve immediately.

CHINESE-STYLE SCALLOPS

VARIATION OF SCALLOPS WITH LEEK CREAM
❋

Peel and julienne 1¾ ounces (50 g) fresh ginger and 2 green onions. Mix 3 tablespoons (45 ml) soy sauce and 2 tablespoons (30 ml) sesame oil. Distribute the julienned ginger over 8 scallops. Place the scallops in a steamer basket and steam for 2 to 3 minutes over high heat. The scallops must remain slightly pearly in the center. Top with sauce, and garnish with the green onions and chopped cilantro and red chili pepper.

SCALLOPS WITH CITRUS BUTTER

VARIATION OF SCALLOPS WITH LEEK CREAM

❋

Place a piece of citrus butter (see recipe 5) and 8 scallops on a plate, or distribute in individual bowls. Arrange in a steamer basket and steam for 2 to 3 minutes. Garnish with shiso shoots. Serve with fleur de sel or regular salt.

CLAMS WITH HERB BUTTER

❖ **YIELD: 2 SERVINGS** • SOAKING: 45 MINUTES • PREPARATION: 15 MINUTES • COOKING: 5 MINUTES ❖

1 pound (500 g) clams
1 tablespoon (15 ml) coarse salt
6 tablespoons (90 ml) herb butter
  (see recipe 4)

1 2
3 4

1	Soak the clams for ¾ hour in cold water with coarse salt.	2	Meanwhile, cut the butter into small pieces so you can easily stuff the clams.
3	Drain the clams then place them in a large steamer basket. Steam for 3 to 5 minutes, just enough time for them to open.	4	Stuff each clam with a piece of herb butter, or invite your guests to do it themselves, as they eat.

STEAMED FISH WITH HERBS

YIELD: 2 SERVINGS • PREPARATION: 10 MINUTES • COOKING: 12 MINUTES

2 garlic cloves
Herbs of your choice (basil, lemon thyme,
   flat-leaf parsley, cilantro, oregano, etc.)

1 lemon
1 whole fish (sea bream, sea bass, red
   mullet or similar), scaled & dressed by a
   fishmonger

Coarse salt & pepper, to taste
1 to 2 tablespoons (15 to 30 ml) olive oil

1 2
3 4

1	Slice the garlic cloves. You don't need to remove the skin.	2	Wash the herbs. Slice the lemon into rounds.	
3	Place the fish on parchment paper. Season with salt and pepper, and slide the garlic slices and lemon rounds inside the opening in the fish.	4	Attach the herbs to the fish using thin twine.	➤

| 5 | Sprinkle a little olive oil over the fish and steam in the paper. A fish weighing about 2 pounds (1 kg) needs to steam for between 10 and 12 minutes. | **TIP**
❀
☛ It's better not to over-steam the fish. If, by lifting the fish, you notice that it is not cooked through, finish cooking in a microwave oven at 3- to 5-second intervals. |

		SAUCES ❋
6	Serve with salt, pepper and lemon.	You can serve the fish with mousseline sauce (see recipe 9), light tartar sauce (see recipe 17), light mayonnaise (see recipe 11) or a flavored butter (see recipes 4, 5, 6 and 7).

CANTONESE FISH

❧ **YIELD: 2 TO 4 SERVINGS** • **PREPARATION: 30 MINUTES** • **COOKING: 15 MINUTES** ❧

1 whole fish (sea bass, brill, sea bream, dab,
   turbot or similar), dressed and scaled
Salt, to taste
Fresh ginger, to taste
1 bunch green onions

1 bunch cilantro
Fresh red chili pepper, to taste
3 tablespoons (45 ml) vegetable oil
1 tablespoon (15 ml) oyster sauce
2 tablespoons (30 ml) soy sauce

PRELIMINARY:
Score and lightly salt the fish.

1 2
3 4

1	Peel and julienne the ginger and green onions. Wash the cilantro and pluck the leaves from the stems. Chop the chili pepper.	2	Place the fish on a dish in a steamer basket, or use a large wok and place a raised grill or a wide can, open at both ends, inside.
3	Steam a 2-pound (1 kg) fish for 10 to 15 minutes.	4	In a small saucepan, bring the oil, oyster sauce and soy sauce to a boil. ➤

	Five minutes before the fish finishes cooking, sprinkle the ginger over it.	**VARIATIONS** ❊
5		You can substitute sesame oil or garlic oil (see recipe 2) for the vegetable oil. You can also add a little rice wine to the sauce.

		SERVING SUGGESTION
6	Once the fish is cooked, drain the water. Top with the sauce, green onions, chili pepper and cilantro. Serve immediately.	For a complete menu, serve the fish with Thai rice and small bok choy in oyster sauce (see recipe 56).

SALMON FILLETS WITH VEGETABLES

⟿ YIELD: 2 SERVINGS • PREPARATION: 20 MINUTES • COOKING: 10 MINUTES ⟻

6 dried shiitake mushrooms
Fresh cilantro, to taste
1 garlic clove
1 ounce (20 g) fresh ginger
2 carrots

2 tablespoons (30 ml) vegetable oil
3 tablespoons (45 ml) oyster sauce
Salt & pepper, to taste
2 large salmon fillets, with or without the
  skin

PRELIMINARY:
Soak the shiitake mushrooms in cold water
until they are rehydrated. Wash the cilantro
and pluck the leaves from the stems.

1	Finely slice the garlic and rehydrated shiitake mushrooms, and julienne the ginger and carrots.	2	Heat the oil. Once it is hot, lightly brown the garlic and mushrooms.	3	When the mushrooms turn golden, add the ginger and carrots. Cook for 2 minutes.
4	Add the oyster sauce and ¼ cup (60 ml) water. Remove from the heat as soon as the carrots are cooked. Season with salt and pepper.	5	Steam the salmon fillets on a plate for 5 to 10 minutes, depending on the size.	6	Place the cooked fish on plates and top with sauce and cilantro leaves.

HO MOK PLA

❖ **YIELD: 4 SERVINGS** • PREPARATION: 30 MINUTES • COOKING: 10 MINUTES ❖

1 package banana leaves
4 kaffir lime leaves
1 pound (500 g) cod fillets
1 scant tablespoon (13 ml) red curry paste
½ teaspoon (2 ml) salt

1 heaping teaspoon (6 ml) sugar
1 tablespoon (15 ml) fish sauce
2 eggs
1 scant cup (225 ml) coconut milk
8 large Napa or Chinese cabbage leaves

1 bunch Thai basil

PRELIMINARY:
Wipe the banana leaves with a damp cloth.
Mince the lime leaves.

1 2
3 4

1	Cut eight 7-inch (17 cm) diameter circles out of the banana leaves. Stack 2 leaf circles, with the veins perpendicular.	2	Fold up the edges of the circles by 1½ inches (4 cm) by making 4 pleats of ½ inch (1 cm) each. Pin with toothpicks.
3	Debone the fillets. Pat them dry and chop into chunks.	4	Mix the curry paste, salt, sugar, fish sauce, eggs and ½ cup (125 ml) coconut milk. Add the lime leaves and stir. ➤

5 6
7 8

5	Add the pieces of fish. Combine well and let rest in the refrigerator.	6	Finely slice the cabbage leaves. Boil for 4 minutes, then wring well, squeezing between your hands. No water must remain on the cooked cabbage leaves.
7	Reduce the rest of the coconut milk by half. Set aside.	8	Fill the bottom of the banana-leaf vessels with cabbage and Thai basil, and then evenly distribute the fish mixture.

9	Steam for 10 minutes. Drain any excess water from the custard and arrange the hok mok pla on a dish or platter. Top with the reduced coconut milk and garnish with the minced lime leaves.	**SERVING SUGGESTION** ❋ Accompany the ho mok pla with Thai rice. **TIP** ❋ ☞ You can cook this mixture in small ramekins or aluminum tart molds instead of the banana leaves.

SHRIMP HO MOK PLA

VARIATION OF HO MOK PLA
❋

Follow the method outlined in recipe 86, but substitute 1 pound (500 g) raw shelled shrimp for the cod fillets. Line a dish or an aluminum tray with cabbage leaves topped with the shrimp mixture. Steam for 10 to 15 minutes, depending on the size of the shrimp.

CHICKEN HO MOK PLA

VARIATION OF HO MOK PLA
❀

Follow the method outlined in recipe 86, but substitute 1 pound (500 g) chicken breast for the cod fillets and green curry paste for the red curry paste. Substitute 7 ounces (200 g) rinsed bamboo shoots for the cabbage leaves. Line a dish or an aluminum tray with the bamboo, top with the chicken and steam for 10 to 12 minutes.

STEAMED CHICKEN WITH SOY SAUCE

➤ **YIELD: 4 SERVINGS** • **PREPARATION: 10 MINUTES** • **MARINATING : 30 MINUTES** • **COOKING: 25 MINUTES** ⬅

1 whole free-range chicken, cut into pieces
Salt, to taste
1½ ounces (40 g) fresh ginger, julienned
  (thin strips)

½ cup (125 ml) Shaoxing or other rice wine
1 small bunch cilantro
1 bunch green onions

2 tablespoons (30 ml) garlic oil
  (see recipe 2) or sesame oil
3 tablespoons (45 ml) soy sauce

1 2
3 4

1	Rub the pieces of chicken with a little salt and ½ ounce (15 g) julienned ginger. Add the wine and let marinate for ½ hour.	2	Arrange the chicken on a plate. Steam for 15 minutes in a steamer basket. Turn off the heat and let rest, covered, for 10 minutes.
3	Meanwhile, wash the herbs. Pluck the cilantro leaves from the stems and finely slice the green onions.	4	Remove the chicken from the steamer basket and arrange on a platter. Top with the garlic oil and soy sauce. Sprinkle the ginger and herbs over top. Serve hot, accompanied by white rice.

COUSCOUS MEATBALLS

➤ YIELD: 6 SERVINGS • PREPARATION: 30 MINUTES • COOKING: 1 HOUR ➤

FOR THE MEATBALLS:
3 ounces (80 g) bread (about 2 to 3 slices)
2 onions • 1 garlic clove
10½ ounces (300 g) ground beef or lamb
1 egg • 1 teaspoon (5 ml) ground coriander
½ teaspoon (2 ml) cinnamon
½ teaspoon (2 ml) pepper
½ teaspoon (2 ml) chili powder

1 teaspoon (5 ml) cumin
1 teaspoon (5 ml) harissa, to taste
½ teaspoon (2 ml) salt
1 small bunch flat-leaf parsley, minced
1 small bunch cilantro, minced
FOR THE STOCK: 3 tomatoes • 3 onions
4 carrots • 4 turnips • 2 zucchini, ½ green
cabbage • 1 slice pumpkin

1 (19-ounce/540 ml) can chickpeas
3 tablespoons (45 ml) olive oil
1 tablespoon (15 ml) tomato paste
1 tablespoon (15 ml) ground ginger
1 tablespoon (15 ml) salt
1 teaspoon (5 ml) ras el hanout
Pepper, to taste • 2 garlic cloves
1 tablespoon (15 ml) harissa

1

2

3

4

5

6

2½ cups (625 ml) Moroccan couscous (not pre-cooked or instant) Salt, to taste Olive oil, to taste	1	Make the meatballs first. Start by soaking the bread in a bowl of water. When soft, wring well.	2	Finely slice the 2 onions. Crush half of the garlic clove, and save the rest for the stock.	3	Coarsely blend the bread, onion, crushed garlic, meat and egg in a food processor.	
	4	Add the ground coriander, cinnamon, pepper, chili powder, cumin and harrisa, and mix well by hand.	5	Add the minced flat-leaf parsley and cilantro. Mix well.	6	Shape the meatballs in your hands. Let rest in the refrigerator.	➤

7 8
9 10

7	Wash, peel and chop the vegetables for the stock. Rinse the chickpeas.	8	Lightly brown the onions in the olive oil. Add the tomatoes, the tomato paste and the ground ginger, salt, ras el hanout and pepper. Cook for 5 to 10 minutes, until the onions are soft.
9	Add the garlic cloves and 1 quart (1 L) water, and bring to a boil. Line the pan with cheesecloth to create a couscous-maker. The liquid in the bottom of the pan should just simmer.	10	Place the couscous in a container, drizzle oil over top and then add 1 scant cup (200 ml) water. Rub the couscous between your hands.

11 12
13 14

11	Pour the couscous into the cheesecloth, distributing evenly. Cook until the steam escapes from the grains.	12	From the time the steam starts to pass through the couscous, cook for another 10 minutes. Do not cover.
13	Transfer the couscous to a bowl. Let cool. Meanwhile, add the carrots and turnips to the stock.	14	Break up any lumps that have formed in the couscous with your hands. Add 1 scant cup (200 ml) salted water. Rub the couscous again in your hands. ➤

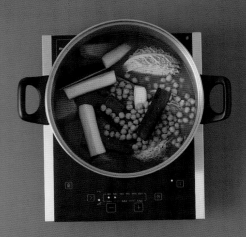

15 16
17 18

15	Return the couscous to the couscous-maker. Cook for 15 minutes from the time the steam passes through the grains.	16	Let the couscous cool. Meanwhile, add all the rest of vegetables to the stock.
17	Fluff the couscous with a fork. Pour 1 scant cup (200 ml) water in the couscous and fluff again by rubbing it in your hands before cooking for a third time.	18	Add the meatballs to the stock, place the couscous on top and cook for another 15 minutes.

| 19 | Check to make sure the vegetables and meatballs are done. Taste the stock and adjust the seasoning, as needed. Arrange the vegetables and the meatballs on a platter. Serve with a bowl of stock and the harissa. | **TIP**
❊
To deepen the flavor of the stock, brown meat trimmings (beef short ribs, chicken wings, etc.) with the onions. Remove before serving. |

DESSERTS

6

STEAMED HONEY CAKE

❧ YIELD: 6 SERVINGS • PREPARATION: 10 MINUTES • COOKING: 35 MINUTES ❧

¼ cup (60 ml) butter
2 eggs
½ cup (125 ml) brown sugar
3 tablespoons (45 ml) honey

1 tablespoon (15 ml) vanilla extract
3½ tablespoons (52 ml) powdered milk
1 cup (250 ml) self-rising flour
½ teaspoon (2 ml) baking soda

PRELIMINARY:
Melt the butter. Let cool.

1
4

2
5

3
6

1	With an electric mixer, whisk the eggs and sugar for 5 minutes.	2	Add the honey, vanilla, powdered milk and melted butter.	3	Whisk until the mixture is uniform.
4	Gradually fold in the flour and baking soda with a spatula.	5	Pour the batter into a 6- to 7-inch (16 to 18 cm) diameter bamboo basket lined with parchment paper and steam for 35 minutes.	6	Remove the basket from the steam, and let the cake cool before cutting and serving.

BANANA FLANS

❖ YIELD: 6 SERVINGS • PREPARATION: 15 MINUTES • COOKING: 15 MINUTES ❖

FOR THE FLAN:
1 pound (500 g) bananas, not too ripe
　(about 3 or 4)
6½ tablespoons (97 ml) sugar
⅓ cup (75 ml) rice flour
3 tablespoons (45 ml) coconut milk

FOR THE COCONUT CREAM:
1¼ cups (310 ml) coconut milk
1 tablespoon (15 ml) sugar
1 teaspoon (5 ml) tapioca flour
1 tablespoon (15 ml) rice flour
Pinch salt

1 2
3 4

1	Mash the bananas with a fork. Add the sugar, rice flour and coconut milk. Mix well.	2	Evenly distribute the banana mixture among small ramekins. Steam for 10 minutes.
3	Meanwhile, prepare the coconut cream. Heat the coconut milk and sugar in a saucepan. Add the flours and salt. As soon as the mixture thickens, turn off the heat and set aside.	4	Wait until the flans are completely cool before topping with the coconut cream. You can also add roasted sesame seeds. Set aside in the refrigerator.

COCONUT-CARAMEL FLAN

❧ YIELD: 6 SERVINGS • PREPARATION: 15 MINUTES • COOKING: 20 MINUTES ❧

FOR THE CARAMEL:
7 tablespoons (105 ml) water
¾ cup (175 ml) sugar

FOR THE FLAN:
4 eggs
6½ tablespoons (97 ml) sugar

1⅓ cups (325 ml) coconut milk
½ cup (125 ml) milk

1 2
3 4

1	Heat the water and sugar in a saucepan. Reduce until you obtain a fairly liquid caramel.	2	Pour the caramel into molds or ramekins, ensuring it covers the sides (and doesn't just sit in the bottom). Work quickly because the caramel will harden quickly.	
3	Whisk the eggs with the sugar.	4	Add the coconut milk and the milk. Whisk to mix well.	➤

| 5 | Fill the molds. |

| 6 | Steam for 20 minutes. Let cool before turning the flans out of the molds. | |

CRÈME CARAMEL

❧ **YIELD: 4 TO 6 PERSONNES** • PREPARATION: 15 MINUTES • COOKING: 10 MINUTES ❧

FOR THE CARAMEL:
½ cup (125 ml) sugar
2 tablespoons (30 ml) water

FOR THE CUSTARD:
3 cups (¾ L) milk
⅔ cup (150 ml) sugar
5 eggs

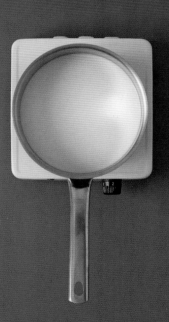

1	Prepare the caramel first, by heating the sugar and water in a saucepan.	2	As soon as the caramel starts to turn golden, take it off the heat.
3	Pour into a mold. Coat the sides of the mold by turning it until the sides are almost completely covered.	4	Bring the milk to a boil.

5 6
7 8

5	Whisk the sugar and eggs together in a bowl.	6	Pour the hot milk into the egg-sugar mixture. Whisk well.
7	Pour the custard into the mold.	8	Place a plate over the mold or cover with plastic wrap. Cook in a pressure cooker for 8 minutes. Turn off the heat and continue cooking under pressure for another 2 minutes.

9 Depressurize. Let cool before turning the crème caramel out of the mold and onto a dish. Serve cold.

VANILLA CUSTARD

❧ **YIELD: 6 SERVINGS** • PREPARATION: 20 MINUTES • COOKING: 15 MINUTES ❧

2 vanilla beans
2 cups (500 ml) milk
5 egg yolks
7 tablespoons (105 ml) sugar

1 2
3 4

1	Split the vanilla beans in half and scrape out the seeds.	2	Heat the scraped pods and seeds with the milk.
3	Once the milk boils, turn off the heat and let infuse for 10 minutes. Remove and discard the scraped pods.	4	Whisk the egg yolks with the sugar until the color lightens. ➢

5	Add the warm milk and mix well. Let rest for 5 minutes. Remove the foam at the surface and pour the custard into ramekins.	**CHIC VARIATION** ❋ Add chips of glazed chestnuts.

		VARIATION
		✿
6	Steam in a steamer basket for 15 minutes. Serve cold.	You can add apple or pear compote to the bottom of the ramekins. Dice the fruit, add a little sugar and cook in a saucepan until the fruit is soft yet still intact.

COFFEE CUSTARD

VARIATION OF VANILLA CUSTARD
❊

Follow the method described in recipe 95,
substituting 2 or 3 tablespoons (30 to 45 ml)
of coffee extract, according to taste, for the vanilla.

MATCHA CUSTARD

VARIATION OF VANILLA CUSTARD
❋

Follow the method described in recipe 95,
substituting 1 heaping tablespoon (17 ml)
of matcha for the vanilla.

APPENDIXES

INGREDIENTS AND COOKING TERMS

TABLE OF CONTENTS

RECIPE INDEX

SUBJECT INDEX

ACKNOWLEDGMENTS

INGREDIENTS AND COOKING TERMS

BAMBOO

Only the shoots of the bamboo plant are edible. Picked as soon as they poke through the ground, they are boiled to remove any bitterness then peeled so only the tender heart remains. Bamboo shoots are available in large supermarkets and in Asian supermarkets. They are available whole, sliced, cubed or julienned in cans or in jars. Rinse well under cold water before using.

BANANA LEAF

Packaged banana leaves can be found in the vegetable section of Asian supermarkets. They can be stored in the refrigerator or freezer. Wipe using a damp sponge before using. If the leaves start to crack, put them in a hot oven for 10 seconds or boil them for a few seconds.

BLANCH

A culinary term generally used for vegetables or fruits. It means briefly plunging in boiling water then plunging in ice water or running under cold water (to stop the cooking process). Cooks blanch vegetables to make them easier to peel, to remove acridity, to soften vegetables or to reduce the volume of some vegetables.

BOK CHOY

Bok choy is Cantonese for white vegetable, but it's a small Chinese cabbage with green leaves! Choose one that is firm and round and without brown spots. You can find bok choy in supermarkets, wrapped in plastic in the fresh produce section or in the vegetable section.

CAUL

Also called caulfat, it is a very thin membrane taken from a pig's abdomen. It's often used to hold together pâtés, roasts, and meats stuffed and rolled, such as for roulades and ballotines. Caul melts when cooked, leaving only the faintest trace, does not change the taste of food and is easy to handle. Soak it in cold water then rinse before using. Caul can be bought from a butcher and is sometimes available pre-packaged in supermarkets.

CHAWANMUSHI

This little salted Japanese custard is usually served as an appetizer. It is made with stock, eggs and a garnish. The stock and the garnish can be prepared in a variety of ways,

including ingredients such as seafood, fish, smoked duck breast, sugar snap peas and celery. In Japan, it's served in a special small bowl with a cover, but you can prepare it in small ramekins.

CHINESE BUN FLOUR

"Special bun flour" or "steamed bun flour" is a special flour mixture to prepare Chinese bun dough. The buns will be whiter and will more closely resemble those found in stores and restaurants. However, this mixture contains whitening agents and is less natural than regular all-purpose flour.

CURRY PASTE

An indispensable condiment of Thai cooking. The ingredients are crushed in a mortar until they're a uniform puree. Red curry paste is made with red chili peppers, shallots, garlic, galangal, lemongrass, cilantro and kaffir lime. Green curry paste is made with the same ingredients, except green chili peppers are used instead of red ones. There is also a yellow curry paste made with turmeric. Curry pastes can be found in the international foods section of supermarkets and, of course, in Asian supermarkets. Once open, place jars or packets of curry paste in the refrigerator.

DASHI

This basic stock is used in a number of Japanese dishes. It is made from kombu (dried seaweed) and flakes of dried, smoked bonito. It can be found in Asian supermarkets, in granular form for immediate use and in bags for infusing. A distinction is made between first dashi, "ichiban dashi," which is very light and is used in sauces and clear soups, and second dahsi, "niban dashi," which is the spicier version. In fact, niban dashi is made by simmering the ingredients of ichiban dashi for longer. Dashi is used to make miso soups, fondues and nabe (Japanese one-pot dishes).

DEGLAZE

Heating and stirring a small amount of liquid, such as wine or stock, in a pan in which other foods, usually meat, have been cooked. Done to dissolve small food particles stuck to the bottom of the pan, usually to use as a base for a sauce.

DIM SUM

This is, in some ways, the Cantonese version of brunch. Traditionally served in restaurants in Hong Kong between 7 a.m. and 3 p.m., it includes a vast array of dishes (dumpling, buns, etc.) presented in small portions. Steamed or fried, salty or sweet, dim sums are accompanied by pu'er tea (meaning semi-fermented), which is supposed to help with digestion. Eating dim sum is referred to as yamcha in Chinese, or "drinking the tea." Indeed, the origins of dim sum go back to the time of the Silk Road. Merchants, exhausted from their travels, would usually stop at itinerant teahouses along the route. Small snacks were served with the traditional hot drink.

ENOKI MUSHROOMS

This mushroom, originally from Asia, grows in bunches and consists of a long stem and a tiny white cap. Enoki mushrooms are sold packaged in the fresh produce section of Asian supermarkets. The enoki tastes sweet and has a slightly crunchy texture. Cut and throw away the base of the bunch then rinse before eating, raw or cooked. It's better to cook enoki mushrooms quickly because the stems can become stringy.

FERMENTED BLACK BEANS

Steamed soybeans that are salted then fermented. It's a process that creates the characteristic color of the beans. Used in China as seasoning, they are packaged and sold in the condiments section of Asian supermarkets.

FISH SAUCE

Called nuoc mam in Vietnamese, it's a sauce made from fermented fish in brine. There are fish sauces based on squid or a combination of fish, but the most prized is the one made exclusively from anchovies.

FROMAGE BLANC

A French cheese that is uncooked, unmolded and unripened, giving it a texture somewhat like cream cheese or Greek-style yogurt. Authentic fromage blanc contains little, if any, fat and has a mild, tangy flavor. Available in specialty food stores.

GALANGAL

This is a rhizome that closely resembles ginger, hence it is sometimes called Thai ginger. It's sold in little packets in the produce section of Asian supermarkets. You can substitute a little ginger and a kaffir lime leaf for galangal.

GREEN ONIONS

Sometimes erroneously called scallions, green onions are simply immature onions. The ones sold in supermarkets are generally quite young and tender, but you can find larger, more mature green onions, sometimes called bulb onions, in farmer's markets and specialty food stores.

GREEK-STYLE YOGURT

Also called strained yogurt, yogurt cheese and simply Greek yogurt, it is plain yogurt that has been strained to remove the whey (the liquid), creating a thick, spreadable product. You can make your own by lining a strainer with cheesecloth, filling with plain yogurt and leaving to drain for a few hours or overnight.

HARISSA

A North African condiment, harissa is a paste made of chilies, oil, garlic, cilantro, cumin and ground coriander, and it also can include dried mint and verbena leaves.

HOISIN SAUCE

A kind of Chinese barbecue sauce, hoisin sauce is brown and thick. It's prepared using fermented soybeans, vinegar, sugar, garlic and various spices. It can be found canned or in plastic bottles, which are more practical to use.

HO MOK PLA

A great classic of Thai cooking, the name literally means "wrap and stuff the fish." Originally from Bangkok, it's a type of fish custard with curry.

JAPANESE GROUND CHILI PEPPER

Called "nanami togarashi" or simply "togarashi," it's a combination of spices: ground chili pepper, orange zest, sesame seeds, ginger, dried seaweed and sansho pepper. It's used to season soups, noodles and yakitori (skewers).

JULIENNE
A culinary term generally used in relation to vegetables. It means slicing into fine strands.

KAFFIR LIMES
A citrus fruit that resembles a small lime with gritty skin. The leaves are sold in the freezer section of Asian supermarkets. Indispensable in Thai cooking, the leaves are used to flavor stock, curries and various dishes.

KING OYSTER MUSHROOM
A rather large mushroom (the size is between a porcini and an oyster mushroom). It has a large stem and can be found at markets and packaged in the produce section of Asian supermarkets.

LEMONGRASS
This is an indispensable ingredient in Southeast-Asian cooking, particularly Thai and Vietnamese. Remove the hard stem and peel the stalks so that only the tender white parts of the heart are left. Lemongrass can be found in the produce section of Asian supermarkets and sometimes in large supermarkets. It freezes well, but place it in a sealed bag because its flavor can taint other foods.

MAKI ROLL
Maki is a term generally applied to sushi rolls (hosomaki and futomaki).

MATCHA TEA
Ground Japanese green tea.

MUSSELS
De-beard mussels by removing any tough, stringy filaments, but only do so just prior to cooking, as de-bearding will kill the mussel. You should discard any raw mussels with open shells that don't close immediately when tapped and any mussels that don't open once cooked.

NAPA CABBAGE
Also called Chinese cabbage, in Mandarin it's called "bai cai," which literally means the white vegetable. Choose a firm one without spots. It can be eaten raw or cooked and can be kept for a week in the refrigerator.

OYSTER SAUCE
This is a thick brown sauce with a pronounced flavor. Made from oysters, cornstarch and caramel, it gives dishes an incomparable taste. It's generally used with vegetables and sautéed dishes but also in marinades. You can find it in the international foods section of supermarkets.

RAS EL HANOUT
A North African spice blend that can contain 20 to 50 ingredients, typically including anise, cardamom, cumin, ginger, cinnamon, cloves, black pepper, turmeric, coriander, nutmeg, chili and dried flowers.

SAUCE CHIEN
Originated in French West India, this Creole sauce is used to accompany fish and grilled meats. The name originally came from the brand of knife used to chop the ingredients.

SHAOXING WINE
Shaoxing wine is made from fermented sticky rice and is used in marinades and sauces. It can be replaced with another rice wine or sherry wine.

SHIITAKE MUSHROOMS
This Asian mushroom takes its name from the shii tree (its host, which is a cousin of the oak). You can find them fresh or dried. Packages of dried mushrooms are practical because they keep longer and you just have to soak them in cold water for 15 to 20 minutes to return them to their original shape.

SHIMEJI MUSHROOMS
This is a small mushroom that grows in clusters or bunches. Cut off the base of the bunch and eat cooked (they will be easier to digest). Shimeji mushrooms can be found in containers in the produce section of Asian supermarkets.

SHISO
Both the leaves and shoots are edible. The leaves are used with tuna sashimi and tempuras in Japanese cooking. The shoots are sold in containers and work well with salads. You can find shiso shoots in organic food stores, specialty food stores and Asian supermarkets.

SOFTENED BUTTER
Butter that is soft but not melted. It can be easily worked with a spatula or spoon. Its texture is soft and creamy. It can be obtained by leaving butter out at room temperature. It is easier to soften butter if it is cut into small pieces.

SRIRACHA

This is a spicy sauce, originally from the port city in Thailand that bears the same name. It was originally served in cheap restaurants located on the beach and accompanied seafood. Today it can be found on the table in most Asian restaurants, and it goes well with dumplings, noodles, fried rice, etc.

STAR ANISE

Shaped like an eight-pointed star, this brown pod has an anise flavor that is slightly more bitter than aniseed. Sold whole and ground in supermarkets with an international foods section and Asian supermarkets.

STEAMING

There are baskets and steamers of all kinds: stainless steel, aluminum, bamboo, electric, pressure cookers and woks in which a dish is placed. Bear in mind that the greater the number of holes, the quicker the food will cook. However, electrical steamers cook foods more slowly. If you prefer to use a pressure cooker, do not cook under pressure in order to be able to control the cooking. Regardless of what type of steamer you use, watch the water level and don't add the food and basket until the water is boiling.

STICKY RICE

A long-grained rice that has a very high starch content. Also called glutinous rice and pearl rice. Available in large supermarkets and Asian supermarkets. (Not to be confused with rice that is sticky because it was poorly prepared.)

SWEAT

A culinary term that means eliminating the water from a vegetable by gently heating it in fat, without changing the color.

TAHINI

Originally from Lebanon, tahini is a roasted sesame seed paste and is used to make hummus. It can be found in the international foods section of supermarkets or in specialty food stores.

TAPIOCA FLOUR

Also called tapioca starch, it is starch extracted from cassava starch. It has a neutral taste and is used as a binder or thickener in sauces, soups, fillings and desserts. You can replace it with cornstarch.

THAI BASIL

It can be found in plastic packages in the produce section of Asian supermarkets. Its stem is slightly purple and its dark green leaves are pointier than those of regular basil. It's easy to distinguish by its aniseed taste, similar to licorice.

WATER CHESTNUT

The water chestnut is a bulb vegetable grown in rice paddies. It resembles little chestnuts and has a thin, brownish skin. The flesh is white, crunchy and slightly sweet. It's used in Asian cooking to add texture to fillings, thanks to its freshness and crunchiness, and is usually peeled and canned. Rinse before using. Water chestnuts will keep for several days in the refrigerator in a sealed container filled with water.

WHEAT STARCH

Sold in Asian supermarkets, wheat starch is indispensable for preparing dough for dim sum dumplings.

WONTONS

These are Chinese dough squares made from wheat flour and eggs, much like Italian pasta (so they can also be used to prepare ravioli). They are sold packaged in the produce section of Asian supermarkets and in specialty stores and some supermarkets. Once the package is opened, cover the rest of the wonton skins with plastic wrap to keep them from drying out and use up quickly. Leftover wonton skins can also be frozen.

WOOD EAR MUSHROOMS

Also called Judas's ear, this mushroom may owe its name to its lobed shape and slightly cartilaginous texture. It's hardly eaten in the West, but it's popular in Asian cooking and widely grown there. It is mostly available dried and sold in packages in Asian supermarkets. Once it's soaked in water, it regains its original shape. Sometimes, the mushroom can be very large with a hard stem. Cut away the stem and keep the soft part. It can be eaten raw or cooked.

TABLE OF CONTENTS

1
CONDIMENTS

3
EASY VEGETABLES

2
DIM SUM

4

PAPILLOTES & STUFFED DISHES

5

SPECIAL SUPPERS

6

DESSERTS

RECIPE INDEX

SUBJECT INDEX

LIGHT RECIPES

PICNIC RECIPES

ACKNOWLEDGMENTS

A thousand thank-yous to my happy epicurean dream team: Pierre Javelle for
his beautiful photos and Marie Mersier for the design.

Thanks to Rose-Marie Di Domenico for her confidence.

Thanks to Audrey Génin for her help, her kindness and for always following up.

Thanks to my friends Vania Nikolcic and Élodie Rambau for their advice and support.

To my Chinese family and my family in Lorraine, for their encouragement, help and love of good food.

To K. and JY. Thank you for always being there. Without you, I would be nothing…

A very big thank you to all the press agents and stores that provided
the paint, dishes, utensils and accessories needed to put this book together.

A special thank-you to Jean-Pierre Deval and to Dibbern, as well as
to Pia Jonglez and Céline at the Ressources boutique.

¿Adónde? (www.adonde.fr)
Alessi (www.alessi.com)
BHV (www.bhv.fr)
Bodum (www.bodum.com)
Brandt (www.brandt.com)
CFOC (www.cfoc.fr)
Chasseur (www.invicta.fr)
Cuisinart (www.cuisinart.com)
Dibbern (www.dibbern.de)
Ekobo (www.ekobo.org)
Guy Degrenne (www.guydegrenne.fr)
Ikat
Kimonoya
Kitchen Bazaar (www.kitchenbazaar.fr)
La Sensitive
Muji (www.muji.fr)
Oxstal (www.oxstal.com)
Plastiques
Ressources (www.ressource-peintures.com)
Terre de Chine (www.terredechine.com)
The Conran Shop (www.conranusa.com)
WMF (www.wmf.com)